INDICATIONS

OF

MIASM

by

Dr. Harimohon Choudhury

Second Edition

B. JAIN PUBLISHERS (P) LTD.
NEW DELHI, INDIA

INDICATIONS OF MIASM

© **All rights are reserved**

No part of this publication may be reproduced, stored in a retrieval system or transmitted, in any form or by any means, mechanical, photocopying, recording or otherwise, without prior written permission of the publishers.

Second Edition : 2005

Price: Rs. 69.00

Published by

KULDEEP JAIN

for

B. Jain Publishers (P) Ltd.

1921, Chuna Mandi, St. 10th, Paharganj,
New Delhi-110 055

Ph: 23580800, 23581100, 23581300, 23583100
Fax: 011-23580471
Website: www.bjainbooks.com, Email: bjain@vsnl.com

PRINTED IN INDIA
by
J.J. Offset Printers
522, FIE, Patpar Ganj, Delhi-110 092

ISBN : 81-7021-351-7
BOOK CODE : BC-2829

Dedicated to

All

Classical Homoeopaths

IMMORTAL HAHNEMANN

Hahnemann's theory rests immovably on eternal laws of nature. It will be as immortal as nature herself and with its creator, Samuel Hahnemann, will remain for ever immortal. With imperishable lettering his name will be inscribed in the history of therapy. The brilliance of his name will cast a light not unequal to that of the greatest intellectual figures of all times. As time passes by, the world will realise more potently what, in his justifiable pride and yet noble modesty, he desired to be the inscription for his final resting place on earth.

Non inutilis vixi !

... Richard Haehl,
"Samuel Hahnemann
His Life and Work",
Vol.-I, P. 436.

WHAT ARE MIASMS

"They (Chronic Diseases – H.C.) must therefore all have for their origin and foundation constant chronic miasms, whereby their parasitical existence in the human organism is enabled to continually rise and grow."

– Hahnemann, 'Chronic Diseases', P.9

"... excessively minute, invisible, living creatures, so inimical to human life, ..." "... millions of these miasmatic animated beings."

– Hahnemann, 'The Lesser Writings', P.758

"... the miasm (that probable) consists of innumerable, invisible living beings in and about the patient ..."

– Hahnemann, Ibid, P.761

"... for the smallest remnant (of chronic disease – H.C.) retains a germ for a renewal of the old ailment."

– Hahnemann, 'Chronic Diseases', P.136

"Hahnemann was the first to perceive and teach the *parasitical nature* of infection or contagious diseases, including syphilis, gonorrhoea, leprosy, tuberculosis, cholera, typhus and typhoid fevers; and the *Chronic Diseases in general*, other than occupational diseases and those produced by drugs and unhygienic living, the so-called drug diseases."

– Stuart Close, 'The Genius of Homoeopathy', P.95

"A misunderstanding of the sense in which Hahnemann uses the word "miasm" has deceived many. It was the word loosely used in his time to express the morbific emanations from putrescent organic matter, animal or vegetable, and sometimes the effluvia arising from the bodies of those affected by certain diseases, some of which were regarded as infectious and others not."

– Stuart Close, Ibid, P.95

"The primary error consisted in regarding Psora merely as a *dyscrasia* or diathesis, which is directly opposed to what Hahnemann taught as we now understand it. Instead of regarding Psora as a dyscrasia Hahnemann *included several of the dyscrasiae* among the morbid conditions and diseases *caused by Psora.*"

– Stuart Close, Ibid, P.94

"Even a cursory perusal of Hahnemann's book on Chronic Diseases will convince anybody that Hahnemann's miasms anticipated bacteria or parasites (i.e. living organism, visible or invisible to the naked eye) of modern Bacteriology."

– B.K. Sarkar, 'Commentary on Organon', P.350-351

"Hahnemann had no microscope but he had a keen analytic mind and phenomenal intuition. He used the terminology of his day which he qualified to suit his purpose and thus made it clear that by the word "miasm" amplified by descriptive terms "infectious, contagious, excessively minute, invisible, living creatures" as applied to cholera – poisoning agent he must have meant precisely what we mean today when we use terms of modern Bacteriology to express the same idea. In fact, the idea of 'Contagium vivum' originated with Hahnemann and he can be hailed as the Father of Bacteriology."

– B.K. Sarkar, Ibid, P.332

"Hahnemann's miasmatic theories have been largely misunderstood, ignored, or thoughtlessly transformed into routines for 'clearing' a case of miasms."

– George Vithoulkas, 'The Science of Homoeopathy', P.134

"For Hahnemann there were *acute* as well as *chronic* parasitic diseases caused by micro-organisms."

– M.L. Tyler, "Hahnemann's Conception of Chronic Disease as by Parasitic Micro-Organisms," P.16

FOREWORD

I feel a great pleasure in writing a foreword to this analytical compilation on Dr. S. Hahnemann's Theory of Miasms in treating acute and chronic diseases. Dr. Harimohon Choudhury, an established practitioner with immense knowledge of homoeo-literature wrote many books on homoeopathy in English, Bengali and also in Hindi needs no introduction. His present compilation needs a bit exposure which I shall venture to make here.

Dr. Hahnemann discovered homoeopathy as a natural law of treating disease, whose simple rules are :

(a) To administer single medicine at a time.

(b) The medicine must be potentised one.

(c) In minimum dose, and

(d) On the basis of the law of similars.

The real implication of the law of similars is – like cures like, the term coined as "Similia Similibus Curentur". This is the natural law of cure for natural disease.

Thereafter he found that, although the cures are smooth and gentle, but not everlasting in some cases. He started investigations, studied many cases, scrutinised case histories of the past and examined thoroughly all the aspects of disease and cure. After a hard labour of twelve years he discovered that there must be suppression of uncured diseases which become the fundamental causes obstructing real cure. These fundamental causes, as he termed, are Psora, Syphilis and Sycosis.

Dr. Hahnemann conceived miasms as two types of infecting agent, Psora infects human being as soon as it touches; Syphilis and Sycosis infect people through impure sexual contact. He described Psora as non-venereal and other two as venereal type of miasms. Bacterial agents have been isolated in cases of Syphilis and Sycosis while Psora can be termed as multi bacterial miasm. Therefore, it stands that miasms are nothing but bacterial infections and at some stage these have been suppressed by antipathic treatment and become the fundamental cause of chronic diseases.

He further observed that Psora as an idiosyncratic state of predisposition acted as a receptive ground and fundamental cause of all sickness. Therefore, Psora is the prime factor of all the diseases including Syco-Syphilitic diseases. So the picture of miasm in the present era is mixed miasms due to vaccines, different immunisations and the present day life style. We cannot come out of this situation.

These phenomena give rise to certain conditions which cannot be said as direct infection by this or that miasm but exhibit signs and symptoms remaining latent or manifested at the secondary stage. These are said to be the miasmatic states. In treating chronic disease one should understand all the aspects stated above.

A few words are to be added regarding theory of chronic diseases. It is the most debated concept of the Hahnemannian doctrine. There were controversies at the beginning and it is still continuing in different forms. Dr. Hughes and Dr. Hering refused to accept the theory of miasms. Subsequently Dr. Hering accepted it through experiences. Dr. Kent said, "Psora is the beginning of all physical sickness..., primitive wrong of the human race, the spiritual sickness". This gives rise to further debate with the concept of bacteriological implication with miasms. The realists conceive miasm as nothing but bacteria with some variation. According to them, it does not depend on laboratory tests but on signs and symptoms – which form miasmatic states indicating particular miasmatic dyscrasia.

Dr. Choudhury's treatise on miasms is very explicitly written in all the aspects with practical suggestion which would help the readers immensely. He described the relationship of miasms with micro-organisms, the correct indication of the particular miasm thereby identifying one from another. He described mixed miasms, vaccinosis, acute miasms, etc., to understand and distinguish them for the purpose of treatment. He has written on the present days' dreaded diseases like Tuberculosis, Cancer, AIDS, etc. for appropriate understanding from homoeopathic point of view. He has compiled lists of drugs under each miasm for the benefit of readers. The learned author has performed a really difficult task by compiling these highly valuable and complex subjects.

It is needless to say that this book will be of use to all the homoeopathic physicians and students alike. I wish everybody will study this book and keep it for reference.

Dr. B.B. Ghose

25th June, 1987
71/2G, Netaji Subhash Chandra Bose Road,
Calcutta - 700 040

PREFACE

Nobody can become a classical homoeopath without a proper perception of the miasms. Hence the doctrine of miasms being the kernel of treating chronic diseases occupies the heart of homoeopathy.

Miasms are nothing but the producer of all sorts of diseases. Disease producing agents were designated as miasms in ancient times. Micro-organisms (including viruses) i.e. pathogens of today and miasms of yesterday are synonymous.

Pathogens or miasms are not the sole but the proximate cause of diseases. Pathogens cannot produce any disease. But their residual poisons, toxins or toxic effects are responsible for the production of diseases. These poisons also cannot create any disease unconditionally if the organisms are not sufficiently disposed and susceptible to the particular poison.

We know that micro-organisms are not generally available in the laboratory test at the secondary state of disease or even when the period of manifestation is over with or without treatment. What we really get is the latent or/and secondary states of disease due to acquired or hereditary toxic pathogenetic effect. So the indications described in the book are not the indications of miasms or microbes. Those are actually the *indications of miasmatic states*. With these indications we can very easily identify each of the miasmatic state of our patients. Hence we are to comprehend these *'Indications'* as the indications of miasmatic states.

But the Hahnemannian doctrine of miasms has been misunderstood and mis-interpreted by a section of homoeopaths of the past and the present ages which created controversy and confusion amongst the homoeopathic society. Unscientific and idealistic mode of thinking is mainly liable for this hazard. I have, with all my limitations, taken the opportunity to study and expound the miasms and their states from the angle of scientific and materialistic outlook. It may illuminate my learned friends indefatigably to endeavour to the CORE of the subject. For, any homoeopathic physician who ignores the miasmatic doctrine cannot eliminate deep-seated chronic ailments.

Avoiding the road of controversy I have tried my best to identify the indications of the miasmatic conditions, especially the chronic ones, so that my friends in the profession can easily find out the character and predominancy of each of the miasmatic states in their patients and select the SIMILIMUM for their radical cure. In doing so I have unhesitatingly taken all necessary guidance and assistance from our great teacher Dr. Hahnemann to respected Dr. P.S. Ortega. Moreover, all of my humble practical experiences based on 32 years of my homoeopathic practice have also been dedicated.

We are well conversant of the fact that the movement for health would not be crowned with success till there would remain obstacles to recovery or health. Subjects of anger, anxiety, grief or tension, penurious and unhygienic mode of living, etc., are all great hindrance to human health. For this reason I have, in the course of my discussion, tried to emphasize on one of the points of paramount importance that : *Today's movement for health is not at all isolated from today's movement for a world free from wars, weapons and exploitations.* In this context we may recall WHO's definition of health : *Health is a physical, mental, political and social state of complete well being and not only the absence of illness or diseases.*

My most respected and senior comrade-in-arms Dr. Benode Behari Ghose has taken painstaking responsibility to make the book more complete by correcting my lacunae and adding his mature wisdom of long 50 years of homoeopathic practice. I dare not thank him, I am indebted to him. Hearty congratulation to Dr. A.M.M. Bahadur Munshi (Dhaka) and Dr. Sreemanta Mitra, my friend and guide, for their kind co-operation in writing the book. Warm congratulations to Dr. Nilratan Pal and Dr. Satchidananda Choudhury for their hearty assistance.

Truth is always relative. So it is to be gradually ever perfected. Over and above, my limitations are limitless. So I shall be highly obliged if my errors are pointed out by my learned friends which will be duly corrected for further perfection of the book in future.

Harimohon Choudhury

Homoeopathy International
115E, Lenin Sarani,
Calcutta - 700 013.

WHERE IS WHAT

1. HAHNEMANNIAN DOCTRINE OF MIASMS

INTRODUCTION

The morbific agents which are causally connected with production of diseases, were designated by a general term "miasm or miasma", during the time of Hahnemann. It was the word loosely used in his time to express the morbific emanations from putrescent organic matter, animal or vegetable and some times the effluvia arising from the bodies of those affected by certain diseases. Hahnemann picked up the term which was current in the medical literature of his time but he adorned the word with a special connotation and denotation and used it accordingly.

Like "The Doctrine of Vital Force", "The Doctrine of Chronic Miasms", is another controversial subject in homoeopathy.

The spiritualist and idealist homoeopaths (like Drs. J.T. Kent[1], J.H. Allen[2], H.A. Roberts[3], J. Paterson[4], etc.) defined the miasm as a "condition, state, predisposition, dyscrasia and diathesis". But homoeopaths of more scientific bent of mind, who are known as materialists, could not be satisfied with the above concept. Amongst

---

1. Kent, J.T.   : "Homoeopathic Philosophy", P. 146-176.
2. Allen, J.H.   : "The Chronic Miasm"
3. Robert, H.A. : "The Principles and Art of Cure by Homoeopathy", P. 180-184.
4. Paterson, J. : "Bowel Nosodes" and "Sycosis and Sycotic Co."

them the names of Drs. C. Hering[5], R. Hughes[6], S. Close[7], G. Boericke[8], Margaret Tyler[9], P. Speight[10] and B.K. Sarkar[11], etc., are worth mentioning. Instead of regarding miasms as "dyscrasiae" they included several of "the dyscrasiae" among the morbid conditions and diseases caused by miasms.

It will not be out of place to mention here that the concept of the latter is more akin to that of Dr. Hahnemann. "Hahnemann was the first to perceive and teach the parasitical nature of infectious or contagious diseases, including syphilis, gonorrhoea, leprosy, tuberculosis, cholera, typhus and typhoid fevers; and the *Chronic Diseases in general*, other than occupational diseases and those produced by drug and unhygienic living, the so-called drug diseases"[12]. Hahnemann emphatically stated, "All Chronic disease of mankind, ... show such a constancy and perseverance, that as soon as they have developed and have not been thoroughly healed by the medical art, they evermore increase with the years, and during the whole man's life time; and they can not be diminished by the strength belonging even to the most robust constitution. Still less can they be overcome and extinguished. Thus they never pass away of themselves, but increase and are

5. Hering, C.	: Quoted by J.H. Allen in his book : "The Chronic Miasms", P. 11-12.
6. Hughes, R.	: "Principles & Practice of Homoeopathy", Indian Edn., P. 32 and "Pharmacodynamics" 6th Eng. Edn. P. 87, 90, 839.
7. Close, Stuart	: "The Genius of Homoeopathy", Indian Edn., P. 89-121.
8. Boericke, Garth	: "Principles of Homoeopathy"
9. Tyler, M.L.	: " Homoeopathic Drug Pictures"
10. Speight, P.	: "A Comparison of Chronic Miasms"
11. Sarkar, B.K.	: "Commentary on the Organon", P. 331.
12. Close, Stuart	: "The Genius of Homoeopathy", P. 95.

aggravated even till death. *They must therefore, all have for their origin and foundation constant Chronic miasms, whereby their parasitical existence in the human organism is enabled to continually rise and grow*[13]. And we know that, "Only living beings grow". For that reason Dr. B.K. Sarkar rightly said, "He used the terminology of his day which he qualified to suit has purpose and thus made it clear that by the word 'Miasm' amplified by descriptive terms" *infectious, contagious, excessively minute, invisible, as living creatures as applied to cholera poisoning agent he must have meant previously what we mean today when we use terms of modern Bacteriology to express the same idea. In fact, the idea of "ontagium Vivum" originated with Hahnemann and he can be hailed as the father of Bacteriology.*[14]

Today it is our foremost duty to perceive the doctrine of miasms scientifically and put the same into our day-to-day practice for the recovery of ailing humanity. If we heartily want to do so we should be free from all prejudices including idealistic fetters. Dr. Phyllis Speight very rightly says, "Any homoeopathic prescriber who ignores the miasmatic theory cannot eliminate deep-seated diseases."

MIASM

"Miasma" is a Greek word. It means stain, pollution, defilement. In general, "Miasm" means : (i) a heavy vaporous exhalation or effluvium formerly believed to cause disease, (ii) obnoxious influence or atmosphere, (iii) an unwholesome exhalation, (iv) polluted material,

---

13. Hahnemann, S. : "The Chronic Diseases", P. 9.
14. Sarkar, B.K. : "Organon of Medicine, with an Introduction and Commentary", P. 332.

(v) putrid vegetable matter, (vi) contagion effluvia from human body, (vii) infective material, (viii) the maggots – the larvae from a fly.

The great Shakespeare also said, "Miasms are the maggots that are born within the brain" (Maggot – grub, worm, the larvae from a fly).

Another great homoeopath said, "By miasm, Hahnemann means germ of disease."[15]

Dr. P.S. Ortega also very rightly says, "This source or germ of suffering and death is positive, demonstrable, and perfectly recognizable. He (Hahnemann – author) called it the Miasm.[16]

"When we say 'miasms' we mean 'causes', the aetiology of acute and chronic diseases."[17]

In this connection we would be deceived if we do not hear what Dr. Stuart Close says, "A misunderstanding of the sense in which Hahnemann uses the word 'miasm' has deceived many. It was the word loosely used in his time to express the morbific emanations from putrescent organic matter, animal or vegetable and sometimes the effluvia arising from the bodies of those affected by certain diseases, some of which were regarded as infectious and others not."

BACTERIA

Bacteria Means :

i)   microscopic organisms,

ii) micro-organisms,

iii) microbes,

---

15. Weir, Sir John : "Science and Art of Homoeopathy"
16. Ortega, P.S.   : "Notes on the Miasm", P. 6-7.
17. Grosso, A.J.   : Ibid, P. 57.

iv) schizomycetes or a group of micro-organisms,

v) a class of microscopic unicellular or filamentous plants, saprophytic, parasitic or autotrophic agents in putrefaction, nitrogen fixation, etc., and the cause of many diseases.

Moreover, miasms or according to modern terminology, micro-organisms, those are belonging to the vegetable kingdom – Bacteria, Fungi and Viruses, or animal kingdom – Protozoa, Helminths, etc., are regarded as the proximate cause of many diseases. In short, we may call all these as "disease producing agents", in one word "pathogen." Whatever the dictionary meaning of the term 'miasm' may be, Hahnemann had clearly specified the meaning as "parasites", "germs", "viruses" and "minute living bodies", etc. in different chapters in his epoch making books "Chronic Diseases" and "Lesser Writings".

History of Bacteriology

The past history of bacteriology is not only essential but very much interesting also. Since long time the attention of the scientists were more centered to the different diseases that bacteria might cause rather than to find out what they were. First of all the name of *Fracostorius* of Verona should be remembered. He put forward his conception of "Contagium Vivum" as the cause of infective disease in the year 1546. Then in the year 1659 *Kircher* recorded the presence of minute germs in the blood of plague patient, *Von Plenciz* believed that diseases had some bacterial origin.

The medical profession bow their heads to the memory of Dutch scientist *Leeuwenhoek* for his invention of 'Microscope' in the year 1676.

This is called primitive microscope. From this period medical profession steps towards the world of objectivism from the world of imagination.

In the middle of 19th century the development of bacteriology started with the revolutionary works of *Louis Pastur* (1822-1895) and *Robert Koch* (1842-1910). Koch discovered the comma bacillus of Cholera only in 1882.

Although Hahnemann had no microscope but more than 50 years before Koch's discovery he was the first to perceive, teach and discover the parasitical nature of all infectious diseases and the *Chronic Diseases* in general in the year 1827 before publication of his famous book "Chronic Diseases." It is all the more significant that Hahnemann recognised the presence of bacteria in epidemic and acute diseases in 1818, more than sixty years before Koch isolated the tubercle bacillus. But the irony of the medical history is that his name was totally omitted from the history of bacteriology. Alas ! this is probably the best reward of this ungrateful medical world.

Long time before the so-called modern medicine could even imagine, Hahnemann classified all the diseases in two groups : (1) Acute and (2) Chronic.

According to Hahnemann, acute diseases are divided into three parts – (a) individual, (b) sporadic and (c) epidemic. He had also given hints of endemic and pandemic character of acute diseases.

Hahnemann divided chronic diseases in two parts :

(a) Diseases with fully developed symptoms and (b) Diseases with very few symptoms. He again divided chronic diseases of category "a" in two parts – (i) Non-miasmatic and (ii) Miasmatic.

Non-miasmatic diseases are again sub-divided into three groups : (i) diseases from living unhygienicaly, (ii) diseases due to continued application of non-homoeopathic drugs in crude forms or drug addictions, (iii) occupational diseases.

Miasmatic chronic diseases are also sub-divided into two parts : (i) *Single disease* by Psora, or Syphilis, or Sycosis and (ii) *Compound disease* by Psoric-Sycotic, or Psoric-Syphilitic, or Syco-Syphilitic or Psoric-Syphilitic-Sycotic. These are also of three different types, i.e., (i) Continued, (ii) Intermittent and (iii) Alternating.

Miasmatic chronic diseases with few symptoms are also divided into two parts :

(i) One-sided diseases are sub-divided into two groups, i.e., (a) diseases with only mental symptoms, e.g., mania, insanity, etc., and (b) Diseases with only physical symptoms, e.g., backache, headache, etc.

(ii) Local diseases which are also sub-divided into two groups, i.e., (a) Surgical and (b) Non-Surgical.

This classification of diseases was the first in its character in the history of medicine which is of paramount importance for treatment and management of diseases. And this is one of the greatest contributions of master Hahnemann.

2. ACUTE MIASMS

Hahnemann has clearly stated that acute, half-acute, half spiritual and fixed miasms are mainly responsible for all acute diseases.

He has more clearly defined that miasm are "germs", "virus", "animated living beings", "living creatures", "excessively minute, invisible, living creature", etc.[18].

It is evident that Hahnemann's miasms are nothing but bacteria and other micro-organisms according to modern terminology.

Dr. Kent defined nature of acute miasm very nicely : "An acute miasm is one that comes upon the economy, passes through its regular prodromal period, longer or shorter, has its period of progress and period of decline and in which there is a tendency to recovery".

Depending on recurrence acute miasms are of two types :

1. Recurring type – Those acute miasms which recur in the same manner more than once in a life-time of a particular person is known as recurring type of acute miasms, e.g., Cholera, Plague, Yellow Fever, etc.

2. Non-recurring type – Fixed miasms are those acute miasms which attack persons only once

---

18. Hahnemann : "Organon Sixth Edn." Aph – 33, 150-156 and "Lesser Writings", P. 337, 383 and 758.

in a life-time, such as – Small Pox, Whooping Cough, Scarlet Fever, etc.

Half-acute Miasm – The micro-organisms of Rabies or Hydrophobia are called half-acute miasms.

Half-spiritual Miasm – The living agents of measles, pox, scarlet fever, etc., are also called half-spiritual miasm. After completing their parasitical existence in the organism for sometime they die out leaving the organism to recover soon if the patient survives by that time.

3. CHRONIC MIASM – PSORA

INTRODUCTION

Although the acute diseases were rapidly and completely cured by application of well selected medicines but it was observed that chronic diseases always had a tendency to relapse in a more or less varied form with new symptoms. It was also seen that in some cases they had reappeared annually with an increase of complaints. This apparent failure after discovering and practising homoeopathy for about 30 years (1790 – 1820 A.D.) Hahnemann had to ponder over this matter seriously which led him to discover the theory of Psora as well as of chronic miasms. It took more than one decade of Hahnemann's life for invaluable experimentation on this subject. He said, "I spent twelve years in investigating the source of this incredibly large number of chronic affections in ascertaining and collecting certain proofs of this great truth which had remained unknown to all former or contemporary observers, and in discovering at the same time the principal (antipsoric) remedies, which collectively are nearly a match for this thousand-headed monster of disease in all its different developments and forms"[19].

Regarding the treatment of chronic diseases at the former stage Hahnemann stated, "Its start was pleasing, the continuation less favourable, the outcome hopeless." He further thought that the following five reasons may

19. Hahnemann : "Organon", Foot Note to Aph. 80.

be held responsible for this failure :

1. The law of similars might not be law of universal application.

2. The number of drugs hitherto discovered were too few to cover all types of diseases that afflict human beings.

3. There might be some defect in application of the law of similars.

4. There might be some omission in ascertaining the totality of symptoms on which the homoeopathic treatment is based.

5. There might be some obstacles overlooked, the presence and non-eradication of which prevented lasting recovery.

Hahnemann took up the discussion in detail and found that out of above five points first four were not mainly accountable for obstacles to lasting recovery of non-venereal chronic diseases. At last after prolonged observations and laborious experimentations he could realise that the fifth point is the root of all evils. It was clearly evident to him after innumerable factual observations of himself and other physicians that an eruption of itch suppressed by faulty practice or one which had disappeared from the skin through other means, was evidently followed in persons otherwise healthy by the same or similar symptoms. He gave a general name to the obstacle inhibiting cure as "Psora". By it he meant the "internal itch disease" with or without eruption on the skin.

The dictionary meaning of the word Psora are as follows:

1. The itch or some similar skin diseases.

2. The itch-mite (Sarcoplas scabii, Sarcoptes hominis or Acaris scabii).

The derivation is Latin and Greek, but it is rather Hebraic in origin, coming through the Greek and Latin. The original Hebrew word Tsorat, means :

"A groove, a fault a pollution, a stigma, after applied to leprous manifestations and the great plagues."[20]

According to Hahnemann Psora is the only fundamental cause and producer of all (acute and chronic) diseases of non-venereal nature. It is the most ancient miasm which produces seven-eighths of all chronic diseases for which it becomes most universal mother of chronic diseases. It is most infectious of all chronic miasms. That is why Hahnemann says, *"Psora is that most ancient, most universal, most destructive* and yet most misapprehended chronic miasmatic disease which for many thousands of years has disfigured and tortured mankind ...."[21]

DEVELOPMENT

The development of Psoric pathogen or miasm may be described as under :

1. Mode of infection

The fluid in the itch vesicles contains the Psoric organism. If that fluid comes in contact with the general skin, the itch mite gets an entry in the organism. The disposition of being affected with it is found in almost everybody and under all circumstances.

---

20. Robert, H.A. : "Principles of Art and Cure by Homoeopathy", P. 184.
21. Hahnemann : "Chronic Diseases", P. 9.

F - 3

2. Internal development

From the moment of touching the skin, they remain no more local. No eruption or itching will be seen on the skin during first few days. It remains unchanged and apparently healthy. After a few days when those have received their complete internal development in the whole organism, the local symptoms break forth.

3. Manifestations of external diseases

Psoric miasms are generally manifested in the following three ways :

a) **Primary Manifestations** – After completion of the internal development, the itch miasms try to alleviate and soothe the internal disease through local symptoms on the skin – the itch-vesicles. The incubation period of psoric miasms generally varies from 6 to 14 days. After lapse of this period a slight or more severe chill in the evening and a general heat, followed by sweat in the following night, the itch vesicles come out. At the beginning they are fine, as if from miliary fever, but gradually spreading on the skin. At first they appear in the infected region. These eruptions are accompanied by a voluptuously trickling itching which compels the patient irresistibly to rub and scratch the itch vesicles. These sorts of rubbing and scratching render temporary relief followed by severe burning for a long period. The itching is frequent and more unbearable in the late evening which continues up to mid-night.

In the beginning the itch vesicles contain watery fluid, which quickly transforms into pus and fills up the tips. Violent rubbing breaks up the vesicles releasing the fluid and furnishes much quantity of material for infecting the surroundings of the patient and also other healthy persons. As long as this eruption remains in its natural form the internal Psora and its secondary manifestations can not break forth. In this state it remains slumbering and latent. These troublesome eruptions act as representative for the internal disease and keep the patient free from secondary ailments. In this stage, the disease can easily be cured by internal application of well selected homoeopathic medicines.

b&c) **Latent and Secondary Manifestations of Psora** – But if instead of doing so it is allowed to progress in its own peculiar course without administration of internal curative medicines and various ointments applied externally to drive away the eruptions, then the whole internal disease speedily aggravates and increases. As a result of suppression of primary manifestation of Psora by local application or by non-homoeopathic internal medicines it is forcefully driven inwards and remains in a dormant state which is dangerous. It is called *Latent Psora*. On the other hand if it is exposed to some exciting or maintaining causes like pox, whooping cough, measles or grief, vexation, shock, fall, trauma and burns, etc., the latent psora, slumbering in the organism awakens and breaks out as numerous severe chronic diseases of psoric character. It is termed as

Secondary manifestation of Psora which is much more dangerous to human life. In this way, due to suppression or palliation of Psoric skin diseases by external or internal treatment with pseudo-homoeopathic drugs the seat of the disease which was concentrated in the external comparatively non-important organ like skin has been forcefully driven to much more important vital organs like brain, heart, lungs, liver, spleen, kidney, especially the central nervous system, endangering whole of the human health and life. Dr. Phyllis Speight very rightly says, "Psora spends its force when suppressed upon the nervous system largely, or upon nerve centres often producing nervous and mental phenomena of a serious character, all ameliorated when an eruption is thrown up on the skin."

SYMPTOMS OF LATENT PSORA
(According to Hahnemann)

HEAD
- Perspiration on the head, in the evening, after sleep.
- Frequent one sided headache even from moderate emotional disturbances.
- Frequent falling out of hair of the head, dryness of the scalp, with many scales.

EYES
- Frequent inflammations of the eyes.

NOSE AND SMELL
- Epistaxis in girls and youths (rarely with older persons), often very severe.
- Frequent or tedious dry or fluent coryza or catarrah or impossibility of catching a cold even from the most severe exposure, even while otherwise having continually ailments of this kind.
- Long continued obstruction of one or both nostrils.
- Ulcerated nostrils (sore nose).
- Disagreeable sensation of dryness in the nose.
- Predisposition to catch cold (either whole body or only in parts like head, throat, breast, abdomen and feet) in a draught (in persons not afflicted with psora, though draughts and damp cold air may not be agreeable to them, they do not suffer any cold or evil after-effects there from), (especially when these parts are inclined to perspiration), sometimes long continuing ailments arising therefrom.

FACE

– Pale face with relaxed muscles.
– Red face with frequent flushes of heat and especially associated with anxiety.

MOUTH

– Dryness in the mouth, at night or in the morning.
– Bad smell from the mouth, frequently or almost constantly, especially early in the morning and during the menses. This is perceived as insipid, mouldy, putrid or sour taste in mouth as if from stomach disorder.
– White, or very pale tongue; more frequently cracked tongue.

THROAT

– Frequent inflammation of the throat.
– Hoarseness with much phlegm in the throat.
– Swelling of the cervical glands (Scrofula).

CHEST

– Frequent attacks of dyspnoea.

STOMACH AND ABDOMEN

– Sensation of emptiness in the stomach (H).
– Insatiable hunger, then again want of appetite.
– Nausea, in the morning.
– The abdomen is often distended (H).
– Cutting pains in the abdomen, frequently or daily (especially with children), more often in the morning (H).

DESIRES AND AVERSIONS

– Repugnance to cooked, warm food, especially to meat (principally with children).

– Repugnance to milk.

BOWEL AND RECTUM

– In children – Frequent discharge of ascarides and other worms, associated with intolerable itching in the rectum.

– Venous knots in the anus, passes bloody stools.

– Passing of mucus from the anus, with or without faeces.

– Itching in anus.

STOOLS

– Hard stools, skips days, knotted often covered with mucus or, nearly always soft, fermenting stools, like diarrhoea.

URINE

– Dark coloured urine.

EXTREMITIES

– Usually cold hands with perspiration on the palms or burning in the palms.

– Cold, dry or foul smelling sweaty feet, burning of soles.

– The arms or hands, the legs or feet, are benumbed.

– Frequent cramps in the calves, the muscles of the arms and hands.

– Painless subsultus of various portions of the muscles here and there in the body.

- Twitching of the limbs on going to sleep.
- Swollen, enlarged veins on the legs, varicose veins.
- Pains as of corns, without any external pinching of the shoes.
- Disposition to crack, strain or wrench one joint or another.
- Cracking of one or more joints on moving.
- Predisposition to strains, even from carrying or lifting a slight weight, often caused even by stretching upwards and reaching out the arms for objects which are hung high (so also multitude of complaints resulting from a moderate stretching of the muscles, headache, nausea, prostration, tensive pain in the neck, the back, the limbs, especially, in the teeth in damp, stormy weather, in north-west and north-east winds, after colds, overliftings, disagreeable emotions, etc.).

SEXUAL ORGANS, FEMALE

- Amenorrhoea, menses may be irregular copious, scanty, early or (too late), prolonged watery, associated with other ailments.

SLEEP AND DREAMS

- Weariness on waking early, unrefreshing sleep. Uneasy, frightful or too vivid dreams.

PERSPIRATION

- Perspiration in the morning in bed.
- Perspiration breaks out easily during the day time, even with little movement (or inability to bring out perspiration).

SKIN

- Predisposition to erysipelas.
- Chilblain, or pains as from chilblains, even without severe cold.
- Unhealthy skin; every little lesion passes into sores.
- Cracked skin of the hands and of the lower lips.
- Frequent boils, and felons (whitlows).
- Dry skin of the limbs, arms, thighs and also at times on the cheeks.
- Rough, scaling spot, which causes occasional voluptuous itching, burning sensation after rubbing.
- Occasionaly single insufferably pleasant but unbearably itching vesicle, sometimes pustular, which burns when rubbed; present on a finger, wrist or in some other places.

MODALITIES

- Pains and complaints return while at rest and disappear when in motion.
- Most of the ailments come on at night, and are aggravated by low barometer, north and north-east winds, in winter and towards spring.

SECONDARY SYMPTOMS OF PSORA

MIND

- Hypersensitive and hyperactive. Hence *Psora is called sensitizing miasm.*
- The mind is hypersensitive and hyperactive to slightest stimuli, both endogenous and exogenous, without any outcome. Full of ideas but no tendency to materialise any of them. A psoric subject may be called a 'sterile philosopher' (J.N.K.).

- Disturbances of the mind and spirit of all kinds (H).
- Melancholy, anxious, mania, sad.
- Weeping mood, this often palliates weak memory.
- Extremely restless. Always in a state of hurry, quick. Time passes too fast or too slow.
- Irritable. Weakness makes the patient irritable.
- Fearful. Easily frightened. Timid, want of self confidence, helplessness.
- Fear of fire, of being alone, of apoplexy, of becoming insane, of darkness, of illness, of death.

(Fear-manifested as anxiety is psoric, manifested as anguish is syphilitic and when manifested as outward expression is sycotic.)

- Moody. Sudden change of mood. Sudden transition from cheerfulness to sadness.
- Full of imaginations, emotions and sensations without any objective basis.
- Sudden anxiety with palpitation of heart.
- Thoughts vanish while reading or writing.
- Delusions of all kinds (P.S.).
- Dissatisfaction, grumbler. Fault finding.
- Disinclination to work.
- Bad effects from grief, shock, emotions and fear.
- Malignant cases have all the miasms present (P).

(Weakness of memory indicates psoric, forgetfulness indicates syphilitic and absent-mindedness indicates sycotic tendency.)

- Psoric attacks of all kinds are better by – diarrhoeas. copious urination or perspiration.

SENSORIUM

- Vertigo and reeling while walking (H).
- Vertigo with roaring in the ears, on closing eyes (H), turning over in bed, on riding in a boat or at sea, with nausea and vomiting or when riding in a street car or in a carriage.
- Vertigo of various types, with frequent eructation (H).
- Dizziness; inability to think or to perform mental labour (H), open air causes dizziness and drowsiness.
- Her thoughts are not under her control.

HEAD AND SCALP

- Headache of various types – frontal, temporal, temporo-parietal and sometimes on the vetex. One sided headache.
- Morning headache. aggravates as the sun ascends and ameliorates as it descends.
- Headache with red face and throbbing. Ameliorated by hot applications, quiet, rest and sleep (R).
- Headache as a result of suppressed or repelled eruptions.
- Great hunger before or during headache.
- Feeling of contraction in the skin of the scalp and the face (H).
- Severe itching of scalp with dryness (P.S.), rarely perspiring.
- Dandruff.
- The scalp is full of dandruff, with or without itching.
- Scales upon scalp.
- It always looks unclean.

- The hair looks as if parched and dry (H), they frequently falls out, mostly in front, on the crown and on the top of the head; bald spots or beginning of baldness of certain spots (H). Hair falling generally worse after acute fevers, accute diseases, abdominal or chest diseases or after parturition.
- Hair dry, lusterless, tangles easily, breaks and splits. Cannot comb hair until it is wet or moistened as it is so dry.
- Hair becomes white in spot, premature greying of hair (P.S.).
- Rush of blood to the head (H).
- Heat in the head (H). Cannot bear much heat on head.
- Cold pressure on the top of the head (H).
- Eruption on the head, tinia capitis, malignant tinia with crusts of greater or lesser thickness.
- Dry eruptions on the scalp with itching.
- Dry eczematous eruptions. Aggravated in open air, evening and heat of bed.
- Ameliorated by scratching but burning and itching follow. These eruptions do not suppurate but dry down and become dead scales (R).
- Noises in the brain, singing, buzzing, roaring, humming, thundering, etc. (H).

EYES AND VISION

- Photophobia; light causes pain in the eyes and they close involuntarily (H). (*Photophobia* is more marked in *Tubercular and Syphilitic* patients.)
- Psoric eye troubles are always accompanied by itching, burning (B) and great dryness.

- Eyelids, are closed especially in the morning, he cannot open them (for minutes, even hours); the eyelids are heavy as if paralysed (H).
- Psoric pains are better by heat and worse morning, when the sun rises towards the meridian (P.S.).
- The canthi are full of pus – like mucus (eye-gum) (H).
- Inflammation of eyes of various types (H). These are accompanied by itching and burning of the lids with great desire to rub.
- Edges of eyelids full of dry mucus (H).
- Cannot look long at anything, else everything flickers before him; objects seem to move (H).
- Visual field shows floating spots as of flies, black points, dark streaks or net works; especially when looking into sun (H).
- Spots before the eyes, this is the characteristic of psora (R).
- Sensation of cold in the eyes (H).
- Cornea appears yellow.
- Dim, opaque spots on the cornea (H).
- Dropsy of the eye (H).
- Obscuration of the crystalline lens, cataract (H).
- Squinting far sightedness or short sightedness (H).
- False vision; diplopia or hemiopia (H).
- The eyes seem to look through veil or mist; the sight becomes dim at certain times (H).
- Night blindness. or blindness by day; he can only see well during the twilight (H).
- Amaurosis; uninterrupted dimness of vision increased finally even to blindness (H).

EARS AND HEARING

- Running from the ear of thin, usually foul-smelling pus (H).
- Hearing is excessively irritable and sensitive. She cannot bear to hear a bell ring without trembling; he is thrown into convulsion by the beating of a drum, etc. many sounds cause pain in the ear (H).
- There are stitches in the ear outwardly (H).
- Deafness of various degrees, even upto total deafness, with or without noise in ears; occasionally worse according to the weather (H).
- Swelling of parotid glands (H).
- Tinnitis (H).
- Crawling sensation and itching in the ear (H).
- Dryness and pulsation in the ear (H).
- Usually of a reflex origin or of a nervous character (P.S.).

NOSE AND SMELL

- Profuse, frequent epistaxis (H).
- Stuffed up nostrils (H).
- Sensation of dryness in the nose, troublesome even when the air passes freely (H).
- Sense of smell acutely, increased, weakened or lost (H).
- Cannot endure odours of any kind. Odours produce nausea, headache and vertigo.
- Polypi of the nose, usually with loss of power of smelling; these may extend through the nasal passages into the fauces (H).

- The psoric cold begins with sneezing, redness, heat, sensitive to touch when blown for sometime; discharges are thin, watery, acrid.

- Boils, vesicles and pimples, etc., in the septum which are painful. The septum is often dry, hot and burning in rhinitis.

   (Hay fever in an expression of syphilis and latent sycosis, very often with a psoric taint (R).

   In lupus of the nose three miasms are usually present (P).)

FACE

- Pale face during first sleep with blue rings around eyes (H).

- Sallow yellowish complexion (H).

- Frequent redness of the face and heat (H).

- Predisposition to erysipelas.

- There may be no appearance of psora – or it may be marked.

- Face pale, sallow, earthy, sometimes eyes sunken with blue rings.

- Red lips, swelling and burning of lips.

- In psoric fevers face becomes very red, hot and shiny.

MOUTH, TEETH, GUMS AND TASTE

- Thrush and stomatitis (P.S.).

- Herpes.

- Sordes about the mouth (R).

- Tongue – white, pale, more frequently cracked. Constant flow of saliva. Bad smell in the mouth.

- Constant intolerable sweet taste in the mouth (H).

Burnt taste only psoric. Insipid, slimy taste (H). Bad taste mostly in the morning (H).

- Sour, sweet, putrid, fetid, bitter taste. Taste perverted.
- Dryness of mouth at night or in the morning.

(Any miasm may have a partial or complete loss of taste.

The natural taste in the mouth is neutral. Any sort of perversion or falsification has a miasmatic basis (P.S.).)

THROAT

- Sore throat. Hoarseness, burning in the throat (H).

DESIRES AND AVERSIONS

- Desires sweets, acids, sour things. Likes sugar, candies and syrup.
- Cravings for unusual things in pregnant state which vanishes after child is born; they are sometimes conveyed to the child (P.S.).
- Desires hot foods and drinks.
- Craving fried and seasoned food.
- Aversion to boiled food.

(The therapeutic value of desires and aversions is very high as they are the basic miasmatic symptoms next in importance to perverted mental phenomena in diseases.)

CHEST : LUNGS

- Burning pain in the chest. Band like sensation about the chest.
- Expectoration, mucus scanty, taste loss.

– Cough dry, teasy, spasmodic and annoying.

– Whooping cough. Asthma. Hoarseness.

– Frequent stitches in the chest, with or without cough.

(We know that psora the sensitizing miasm mainly creates disorder of sensation and function. Hence psora itself gives us no physiological change of structure, another miasm must be present in order to procure a physiological change in the structure or shape of a part or organ.)

– Frequent attacks of dyspnoea (H).

CHEST : HEART

– Heart troubles from fear, disappointment, mental shocks, loss of near relatives and friends, or overjoy. These patients think they have heart disease and are going to die.

– Anxiety, fear of heart troubles.

– Sensation of weakness, goneness, fullness, heaviness and soreness about the heart.

– Violent palpitations with beating of the whole body.

– Violent hammering and beating about the heart due to reflexes, such as – gastric troubles, flatulence and uterine irritation.

– Heart troubles from eating and drinking, usually worse evening soon after eating or during digestion. Better – eructations of gas but worse on going to sleep and lying on back.

– Neuralgic pain about the heart.

(Remember that psoric heart diseases are mostly functional. So they will be accompanied with much anxiety, mental distress, with palpitation and neuralgia, often of a sharp, piercing, cutting and stitching nature; worse least movement, at night.)

F - 4

- Psoric heart patient worries about his condition, takes his pulse frequently, fears death and remains quiet.
- Bradycardia (slow pulse) is psoric. Irregular pulse is syphilitic and tachycardia (rapid pulse) is sycotic.

STOMACH AND HUNGER

- Nausea. Vomiting. Hiccough.
- Ravenous hunger. Hunger at night.
- Always hungry, even with a full stomach, weak, 'all-gone' sensations.
- Want of appetite.
- Craving for sour, sweets and acids.
- Repugnance to cooked, warm food, especially to boiled meat.
- Sensation of coldness in the pit of the stomach.
- Pressure in the stomach. Beating and pulsation in the stomach, even when fasting.
- Griping pain in the stomach. Perspiration during eating (H). Eating makes him sleepy.
- Ravenous hunger (canine hunger), especially early in the morning; has to eat at once or he feels like fainting, exhausted and shaky, or if in open air he has to lie down (H).
- Ravenous hunger with rumbling and grumbling in abdomen (H).
- Hungry, but little food causes early satiety & fullness (H).
- Appetite without hunger, swallow hastly without any craving for them (H).
- When she wants to eat she feels fullness in the chest and her throat feels as if full of mucus (H).

- Want of appetite; writhing in the stomach urges her to eat (H).

- Hunger at night. Hunger with weak, gone sensation. Constant gnawing at the pit of stomach.

- Fullness, bloating, great distension due to accumulation of gases.

- Rumblings, gurglings due to formation of flatulence in the stomach and entire gastro-intestinal tracts.

- Sensations of coldness or heat, weight, fullness, tightness, heaviness as if a stone or lump in the stomach after eating. Sensation of beatings, pulsations, throbbings, constriction, oppression after eating.

- Shortness of breath, vertigo, giddiness, anxiety, epigastric tenderness, perspiration after eating. Falls asleep, cannot keep awake after a meal.

- Eating causes pain, colic, nausea, vomiting or is followed by diarrhoea or many kinds of gastro-intestinal diseases.

   (Psoric patients can digest meat better than the sycotic patients.)

- Temporarily better by eating.

- Better by hot drinks and hot application, belching of gas and gentle motion.

ABDOMEN

- Abdomen feels full after eating, often accompanied by a feeling of fullness or distention.

- Pressure in the abdomen as from a stone (H).

- Hardness of the abdomen, it is distended by flatus.

- Tired, sleepy, as if intoxicated, headache, palpitation of the heart after meals.

- Empty, gone sensation in abdomen generally after eating.
- Pain in the liver, hypochondrium and epigastrium.
- Pain in abdomen just after eating. Better by heat and gentle pressure.
- A clucking, croaking and audible rumbling and grumbling in the abdomen. Worse night. Better heat.
- Pressure intolerable.
- Beatings, throbbings, rumblings and gurglings in the abdomen soon after eating and drinking.

BOWELS AND INTESTINAL TRACT

- Psoric patients are mostly hungry and they eat beyond their capacity of digestion and suffer from diarrhoea of various types.
- Watery, undigested, offensive morning diarrhoea (Aloe, Podo., Psorin, Sulph., Tub.). Diarrhoea with no exhaustion (Ph-ac.).
- Diarrhoea due to fright, bad news, or any ordeal, etc., from cold exposure.
- Itching of rectum due to worms. Itching of anus. True psoric stool may be of any colour, generally offensive and not very painful. It is worse by cold, motion, eating and drinking cold things; better by warm drinks, hot food, warm application to abdomen.
- Worst forms of constipation or inactivity of the bowels. No desire for stool. Stool is hard, dry, scanty, difficult to expel.
- Alternative constipation and diarrhoea. Morning diarrhoea.
- Constipation with remote pains – such as headaches, pain in the liver.

- Constipation, stool dry, scanty, hard, difficult to expel.
- Constipation with basilar or temporal headaches, drowsiness, sleepiness, stupor and heaviness, with no desire to work.
- Looseness of bowels gives a weak and languid feeling which is better when constipated (R).
- Tape-worms, pin-worms, round-worms.
- Pale, grey, green and clay coloured stools. Stools hard, semi-solid or watery.
- Bleeding piles, blind piles.
- Polypi in the rectum (H).

URINARY ORGANS

- Retention of urine in children, body becomes chilled. Painful retention of urine, with children and old people. In old people, great distension of bladder with fullness as if extremely full; sense of constriction.
- Frequent involuntarly urination, while sneezing, coughing or laughing and also during sleeping.
- Dark urine. Yellow, brown, whitish, blackish urine. Bloody urine, hematuria, or blood particles in urine (H).
- Fibrous changes in kidneys.
- Many urinary cases are due to reflexes, other disease states, or secondary causes, especially in women.
- Burning and smarting after urination.

SEXUAL SPHERE

- Amenorrhoea, irregularities in menses, it may be copious, scanty, too early (too late), or too long duration, watery, associated with various bodily ailments (H).

- Delayed puberty, appeas after the fifteenth year and later, or after appearing one or more times, they cease for several months and for years (H). Menses of very fetid blood (H).
- Polyp in the vagina (H).
- Leucorrhoea of various types.
- Dysmenorrhoea shows itself very early, at puberty and at climacteric. Pains are usually sharp but never colicky.
- Nightly discharge of the genital fluid in women with voluptuous dreams.
- Nocturnal passing of semen, too frequent, one, two or three times a week, or even every night (H).
- Semen passes off almost involuntarily in day time with little excitation, often even without erection (H).
- There is never a complete erection, even with the most voluptuous excitement (H). One or both the testicles chronically swollen, or showing a knotty induration (sarcocele) (H).
- Dwindling, diminution, disappearance of one or both testicles (H).
- Erections – incomplete, short or lacking.
- Induration and enlargement of the prostatic gland (H).
- Lack of sexual desire in both sexes, either frequent or constant (H).
- Sterility, impotence, without any original organic defect in the sexual parts (H).

UPPER AND LOWER EXTREMITIES

- Pains – Neuralgic type, pains are usually better by quiet rest and warmth and worse by motion.

- Hands and feet dry, hot, often with burning sensations in palms and soles.
- Numbness of extremities.
- Cramps in lower extremities in calves of legs, in feet, toes, ankles and insteps.
- The psoric patient can walk well but it kills him to stand (P).

SKIN

- The characteristic of psoric skin is intense itching and burning. Itching is more frequent and more unbearable, late in the evening, before midnight, heat of bed and undressing. Psoric skin is generally dry, rough and unwashed with or without little pus and blood.
- Nettlerash, pimples, herpes, crusts small, round and red spots on the skin.
- Yellowness of the skin.
- Warts on the face, the lower arms, the hands, etc.
- Whitlow, paronychia, chilblains, corns and boils. Pruritus. Eczema. Anhidrosis.
- Vesicles of the itch – Voluptuous, tickling, itching, patient rubs and scratches, better for a few moments immediately after which there is a long continued burning of the affected parts.

SLEEP

- As soon as he closes his eyes, all manner of phantastic appearances and distorted faces appear (H).
- Very vivid dreams, as if awake; or sad, frightful, anxious, vexatious, lascivious dreams (H).

g and screaming, during sleep (H).

limbs on going to sleep.

ism.

- ... during the day, especially after meals (H).
- He passes the night in a mere slumber (H).
- Weariness early on awakening, unrefreshing sleep.

MALIGNANCY

- The malignancies of psora are prone to develop at the age of 40.

SUPPRESSIONS

- When suppressed psora spends its force upon the nervous system or upon the nerve centres, often produces nervous and mental phenomena of a serious character, all ameliorated when an eruption is thrown up on the skin (P.S.).

MODALITIES

- Aggravations – Standing, heat of room, after eating, new moon, approach of menses, sunrise to sunset, suppression of skin disease and discharges. After eating, after sleep.
- Amelioration – Walking, lying down and being quiet, slow movement, heat, weeping, reappearances of skin disease and natural discharges.

PSORIC MIASM – SUMMARY

1. Psoric miasms of ancient times and pathogens of non-venereal skin or itch diseases of today, the streptococcus and/or staphylococcus, etc., are all synonymous. Psoric pathogens were designated by Hahnemann as '*itch mites*'.

2. These pathogens mainly *produce disorder of sensation and functions* in the organism. Hence these are called the sensitizing miasm. Being sensitizing miasm psora produces almost no structural change but mainly functional disorders, manifested by hypersensitivity, itching, irritation, burning, utmost upto congestion and inflammation.

3. Psora mainly develops the itch or itching papule. Burning, congestions and inflammations are the other imperative phenomena of psora.

4. We can recognize psora by lack, scant or deficiency in one hand and by hypersensitivity or hyperactivity on the other. Psoric is timid, fearful and helpless in one hand and extremely nervous, restless and irritable on the other. Psora reacts to slightest stimuli, both endogenous and exogenous. But funny thing is that it produces nothing. Subject is full of ideas but no tendency to materialize any of them, he is a sterile philosopher.

Psora is characterized by deficiency, various forms of inhibition – "in lacks, in weakness, in inferiority complex, in coldness, in all that LIMITS the individual's expression and given his signs and symptoms a bluish hue." – P.S.O.

INDICATIONS OF PSORIC
MIASMATIC STATES

Now let us try to be more practical in ascertaining the presence and indications of psoric state in a particular individual.

i)   Hypersensitivity. For its extraordinary sensitivity it is called the sensitising miasm. Psora mainly creates disturbance in sensations and functions.

ii)   Man with psoric nature is belonging to the world of outward things. He cannot materialise what he thinks. He may be called a ragged or a sterile philosopher. So the second indication of psora is to thoroughly externalise the human mind. He is utterly a theoretical man with little or no practice at all.

iii) Restlessness. Psoric subject not find peace and is always in a hurry.

iv)   Psoic subject continually changes character. He does not only want to change but every time he wants new things.

v)   Self-centeredness. He is extremely miser and selfish. He has no love and pity for anyone. There may be no affection in psoric patient.

vi)   Psoric subject has hide and seek nature. Mostly psoric patient is dishonest. Privacy, wickedness and impurity play a good deal in him.

vii) Though he is extremely sick but thinks he is all right. Lacks inclination for being cured.

viii) Filthy and timid. Cold and slow.

ix) Redness of all mucous membranes.

x) Where there is psora there must be skin affection or a history of skin disease of psoric nature.

xi) All pains of Psora are generally of neuralgic type. (Bone pain indicates syphilis and joint pain is the indication of sycosis.) Sore, bruised and pressive pains are psoric. (Burning, bursting and tearing pains are syphilitic, stitching, pulsating and wandering pains indicate sycosis.)

xii) Nervousness is the one of the main characteristic of psora. So, where nervous system is affected we think of psora.

xiii) Standing is the worst position for psora. So when we observe that all symptoms are aggravated by standing we think of psora.

xiv) Amelioration by natural discharges is another phenomenon of psora.

xv) *Deficiency,* or *insufficiency,* or *want,* or *scanty* is a great indication of psora. Insufficient morals, courage, discharges, eruptions are all best token of psora. Most of the so-called deficiency diseases originate from psora. Psora produces inflammation.

xvi) Burnt taste in the mouth is an indication of psora. "Burnt taste is ONLY psoric". Sweet taste, insipid and slimy tastes indicate psora.

xvii) Burning is a great indication of psora. Burning of vertex, soles, palms and even whole body. Better by cool air but worse by cold water and bathing as the patient is generally chilly. In tropical countries most psoric patients are hot, desire bathing and feel refresh by that.

xviii)The malignancies of *psora* are prone to develop after the age of 40.

(*Syphilitic malignancies* develop at the age of 40. *Sycotic* malignancies can develop at any age.)

xix) *Psora* develops the itch. (Syphilis the virulent open ulcer and Sycosis the catarrhal discharge.) Unhealthy skin with itching and burning represents psora. (Ulcerated skin with pus and blood represents syphilis, oily skin with thickly oozing and copious perspiration represents sycosis.)

xx) Suppressed psora spends its force on nervous system largely, or upon nerve centres, often producing nervous and mental phenomena of a serious character, all ameliorated when an eruption is thrown upon the skin.

OTHERS :

Psora disturbs metabolism of the element of the lower atomic weights, which are concerned with nutrition (R).

All 'hypos' are mainly psoric. Dyses are syphilitic and 'hypers' are sycotic. Hypoplasia is psoric. (Dysplasia is syphilitic and hyperplasia is sycotic.)

Atrophy is psoric. (Dystrophy is syphilitic and Hypertrophy is sycotic.)

Hypotension indicates psora. (Irregular one indicates syphilis and hypertension indicates sycosis.)

Lack denotes psora. (Deviation syphilis and exaggeration or excess denotes sycosis.)

Weakness is psoric. (Ataxia is syphilitic and restlessness is sycotic.)

Inhibitory quality is psoric nature, destructive quality is syphilitic and expensive quality is sycotic nature.

Psora tends to disturb the nutrition of the whole organism causing tendency towards emaciation, as it affects the metabolism of the formative elements.

Psora prefers the tissues of ectodermal origin.

Blue, the cold colour correspond to Psora. *(Yellow,* the loud colour to Sycosis, and *red,* to Syphilis (P.S.O.).)

Timidity is usually psoric. (Ostentation or fatuousness is sycotic and the desire to kill is syphilitic (P.S.O.).)

Slow intestinal peristalsis is psoric. (Accelerated, exaggerated is sycotic but when it will be perverted into dysenteric spasm will be a syphilitic condition (P.S.O.).)

All the three constitutions of Grauvogl may be classified as under :

The Carbo – Nitrogenoid constitution, is characterised by an excess of carbon and nitrogen, equals psora, the Oxygenoid constitution, is characterised by excess of oxygen, equals syphilis and the Hydrogenoid constitution, is characterised by excess of hydrogen, equals Hahnemann's Sycosis. (Clarke)

Constipation is primarily psoric. (Diarrhoea sycotic and dysenteric spasm is syphilitic (P.S.O.).)

Dryness of a mucous membrane denotes psora, [Augmented secretion denotes sycosis, and ulceration or destruction denotes syphilis (P.S.O.).]

It will be very much easy for us to comprehend patients with predominating *psoric nature* if we can grasp and perceive the above indications of psora.

ANTI-PSORIC REMEDIES

There are more than one hundred antipsoric remedies in our materia medica. But the following remedies are generally known as 'A' Grade antipsoric medicines :

Ars., Ars-i., Aloe., Apis, Hep., Lach., Lyc., Nat-m., Nit-ac., Psor., Sel., Sep., Sulph., Tub., Zinc.

In general the following medicines are considered as antipsorics :

Abrot., Acet-ac., Agar., Aloe., Alumin., Ambr., Am-c., Anac., Ant-c., Apis., Arg-met., Arg-n., Ars., Ars-i., Aur-i., Aur.

Bar-c., Bell., Benz-ac., Berb., Borx., Bufo.

Calc-p., Caps., Carb-an, Carb-v., Cist., Clem., Cocc., Con., Crot-h., Cupx.

Dig., Dulc.

Ferr-m., Ferr-p., Fl-ac.

Graph.

Hep.

Iod.

Kali-b., Kali-c., Kali-i., Kali-p., Kali-s.

Lac-c., Lach., Led., Lyc.

Mag-c., Mag-m., Mang., Mez., Mur-ac.

Nat-s., Nat-c., Nat-m., Nit-ac.

Petr., Phos., Phos-ac., Plat., Plb., Psor., Pyrog.

Sars., Sec., Sel., Sep., Sil., Stann., Staph., Sulph., Sul-ac.

Tarent., Ther., Tub.

Zinc.

4. CHRONIC MIASM – SYPHILIS

DEVELOPMENT

The second chronic miasm is known as syphilis. It is one of the venereal diseases. After an impure coition the chancre appears in the place first infected, usually between the seventh and fourteenth days (the incubation period is 7 to 14 days, rarely earlier or later), mostly on the person infected with the miasm, i.e. *Treponema pallidum*. It appears first as a little pustules, which changes into an impure ulcer with raised borders and stinging pains; if not cured, it remains standing on the same place during man's life-time, only increasing with the years, while the secondary symptoms of the syphilis cannot break out as long it exists. It is also to be noted that the venereal infection of the whole body commences from the moment of the impure coition and is completed before the appearance of the chancre.

If the chancre is removed by local or external application by means of corroding, cauterizing and dessiccating substances then it is followed by the bubo which is a more painful and troublesome substitute. If this bubo is removed through injurious treatment, which is generally done by the allopaths, the nature finds itself compelled to develop the malady by means of more troublesome secondary ailments, through the out-break of the whole chronic syphilis. In this way allopaths injure the patients which is a grave and serious mistake.

Dr. Hahnemann directs us to treat the syphilitic patients having chancre (or the bubo) *in the first simple state* by the minute doses of the best mercurial remedy, in order to cure thoroughly and forever the whole syphilis with its chancre, within fourteen days. We have another great antisyphilitic remedy, *Syphilinum.*

When there is no underlying psora, and if we treat the patient as stated above he will be definitely cured leaving not the least scar but the healthy skin.

In the *second state,* when syphilis is not complicated with developed psora but the chancre (or the bubo) is removed by local application then also all outbreaks of secondary ailments may be avoided and the patient may be cured from every trace of the venereal disease by proper antisyphilitic treatment and its completion will be recognised by the same signs.

But when syphilis becomes complicated with psora that is the most difficult of all these cases. It is designated as the *third state.* This state is also called a *masked, spurious syphilis.*

This complication may be developed in the ways as described below :

(1) When the man at the time of infection was already laboring under a chronic disease (psora), so that his syphilis was complicated with psora, even while the chancre yet existed.

(2) When, even while there was no chronic disease in the body at the outbreak of the chancre, and the indwelling psora could only be recognised by its tokens, an allopathic physician has destroyed the local symptom, not only slowly and with every painful external applications, but has also subjected him for a long time to an internal treatment.

Violent treatment weakens and strongly affects him and as a result general health has been undermined. Psora which has yet been latent within him has been brought to its development and has broken out into chronic ailments, and these impressibly combine with the internal syphilis, the local symptom of which had been at the same time destroyed in such an irrational manner. Psora can only be complicated with the venereal disease when it has been developed and when it has manifested itself as a chronic disease; but not when it is latent and slumbering. In this complicated condition *"it is impossible to cure the venereal disease alone."*

Dr. Hahnemann advised us to treat these patients in the following manner :

(1) All harmful influences that affect the patient should be avoided.

(2) A light and yet nourishing and strengthening diet should be given.

(3) Let the patient first be given the anti-psoric medicine which is homoeopathically best fitting on the basis of totality of symptoms.

When the action of the first medicine completed, probably a second suitable medicine, if required, should be applied on the basis of the totality of prominent symptoms of psora.

(4) Then anti-syphilitic treatment should be given to act against the venereal disease for three, five to seven weeks, i.e. so long as it will continue to produce an improvement in the venereal symptoms.

(5) In inveterate and difficult cases, however, this first course will hardly accomplish all that is desired. Some ailments will still remain which cannot be definitely classed either as purely psoric or syphilitic. These require some additional aid like repetition of a similar process of treatment :

First – another administration of one or more of the anti-psoric remedies that have not yet been used and which are homoeopathically the most appropriate, until whatever seems unsyphilitically morbid, i.e. psoric, may disappear.

Second – then already administered antisyphilitic remedy, but in changed potency, should be applied and allowed to complete its action, until the manifested venereal symptoms of various types have entirely passed away.

"But since these secondary venereal symptoms are so changeable that their temporary disappearance gives no certainty of their complete extinction, we must also wait for that more conclusive sign of the complete extirpation of the venereal miasm afforded by the return of the healthy color and the entire disappearance of the discoloration found in the scar which remains after the extirpation of the chancre by local, corrosive applications."

When syphilis becomes complicated with developed psora and sycosis, the treatment should be given in the following way :

(1) Psora should be treated with antipsoric medicines first.

(2) Secondly, either the syphilis or the sycosis should be treated with the antisyphilitic or

antisycotic medicines on the basis of the predominant symptoms of one of them.

(3) Thirdly, the last one should be treated by well-selected antimiasmatic medicines.

(4) Fourthly, the remaining psoric symptoms had then still to be combated with proper antipsoric medicines.

(5) Lastly, what there yet remained of sycosis or syphilis, should also be treated by means of antisycotic or antisyphilitic remedies as the case may be.

In this connection it is also to be noted, "The complete cure of sycosis which has taken possession of the whole organism before the outbreak of its local symptoms, is demonstrated, like that of the syphilis, by the disappearance of the discoloration of the spot on the skin. Discoloration remains after local destruction of the figwart as a sign of the unextirpated sycosis."

SYMPTOMS OF LATENT SYPHILIS

MIND

– Melancholia.

– Depression.

– Perception is very weak. Memory and power of retention are also diminished.

– Suspicious.

– Introvert. Does not like company, wants to be alone.

– Fixed ideas.

– Strong suicidal tendency : loathing of life, always seeks the chance for committing suicide.

– Suppressive : wants to conceal everything, even does not want to express his/her own suffering.

HEAD

– Hair dry like tow or hemp from an old rope.

– Hair very oily and greasy.

– Falling of hair on sides of head and vertex. Falling of hair in bunches or in spots usually beginning on the vertex.

– Dandruff with thick yellow crusts.

– Head and ears are large in comparison to his body.

– Rolling of the head from side to side during sleep.

– Fetid, sour, oily child.

NOSE

– Flat or depressed nose.

– Diminution or loss of sense of smell.

FACE

- Hard acne on face.

TEETH

- Crowns of incisors become crescentic.

NAILS

- Spoon-shaped and paper-thin nails.

CRAVINGS AND AVERSIONS

- Complete aversion to meat.
- Craving for sour, sweet, chalk, wine, pencil, lime, etc.

AGGRAVATION AND AMELIORATION

- All sufferings are aggravated at night. Hence the patient eagerly awaits sun rise.
- All complaints are aggravated by heat and ameliorated by cold.
- Leucorrhoea or any abnormal discharge ameliorates, but natural excretions like sweat etc., aggravate.

SECONDARY MANIFESTATIONS
OF SYPHILIS

MIND

- The latent syphilitic patient is dull, stupid, heavy and obstinate.
- Oppression and anxiety at night.
- Depressed. Obstinate.
- Fixed ideas and moods.
- Restless, mental spells; patient is driven out of bed with suicidal inclination. The syphilitic patient keeps his depression to himself. The first thing you know is that he has committed suicide. Desire to escape, to get away from self. This often drives them to suicide (P).
- He is a close mouthed fellow. He does not worry his friends with his troubles. He will regard both the death of an individual and the explosion of a nuclear bomb over a town as appropriate.
- All symptoms are aggravated at night and by perspiration.
- Patients become melancholy and condemn themselves (R).
- Morose. Mistrustful.
- Desire to kill and to commit suicide.
- Slow in reaction. Imbecility. Cruelty. Jealousy.
- Idiocy. All quickness of thought is gone and there is a gradual incapacity for understanding things – and this makes him morose. In course of time his mind fails to travel from subject to subject, a quickness that is so prominent

in psora. Thus he grows into one lacking attention and comprehension. If he reads a line he cannot understand its meaning and he has, therefore, to read it over and over again. The mind grows slow - as if paralysed (B). Thoughts and ideas vanish away and he has not the mental ability to bring them back. He reads but cannot retain it; there is a kind of mental paralysis – he forgets what he is about to utter (P).

(This is sometimes seen in tubercular children all through school days and often we attempt to whip them into line but it is constitutional treatment they need (P).)

In basilar meningitis suppression of both syphilis and sycosis induces all forms of mental aberrations. The degeneration and all his kin is either sycotic or syphilitic – usually sycotic, or deeply impregnated with a sycotic taint or a syco-psoric one (P).

– Mischievous, malicious and hatred. (Syphilis precedes psora - P.S.O.).

– Forgetfulness (P.S.O.).

– Prostration of mind.

SENSORIUM

– Vertigo beginning in the base of the brain is more apt to be of a sycotic or syphilitic nature or may be of tubercular origin.

HEAD

– Headache at night. Worse at night or approach of night. They improve in the morning and remain better all day until evening when they grow worse as the night advances, then they grow better towards morning.

- Dull, heavy or lancinating, constant or persistent. Usually basilar or liniear or one-sided.

- Headaches worse on lying down and at night. Generally basilar headache, worse at or after midnight (P).

OUTER HEAD

- Falling of hair from lashes and eyebrows.

- Hair falls out from beard due to skin eruptions.

- Moist eruption in hair.

- Hair fetid, oily, sour smelling.

THE SCALP

- Moist thick crusts.

- Moist eczematous eruption about scalp.

- A thick, yellow, heavy, crust is apt to be tubercular or syphilitic in origin.

EYES AND VISION

- This makes serious inroads upon the structure of the eye.

- Ciliary neuralgia. Ciliary blepharitis is either syphilitic or tubercular.

- Arthritic or rheumatic eye troubles are worse night or after sun sets and worse heat.

- Syphilitic and tubercular patients dread artificial light more than sunlight, although they may be aggravated by both.

EAR

- All organic ear troubles are either syphilitic or tubercular.

NOSE AND SMELL

- Loss of smell. Snuffles in children. It may be sycotic also.
- Ulceration, thick crust (clinkers) often filling whole nasal cavity. The crusts are dark, greenish black or brown, thick and not always offensive.
- Bones of nose destroyed.

FACE

- Face, greyish, greasy appearance, with high cheek-bones and thick lips.
- Deep fissures in lips.
- Moles and papilomas.
- Grey, ashy appearance on face of an infant. It looks old, puckered, dried up, wrinkled like an old man.
- In some cases the skin of the face is rough, voice coarse, deep, often hollow, eyelids red, inflamed, scaly, crusty lashes, broken, stubby, irregularly curved and imperfect. In these cases the *syphilitic* or *tubercular* element predominates in latent form (P).

MOUTH

- Syphilis and tubercular miasms create true ulcer in the mouth.
- Swelling and induration of glands, pathological changes taking place in the teeth or dental arches are of syphilitic or tubercular diathesis. (P).

TASTE

- Saliva is ropy, cottony, viscid, metallic or copper tasting.

 (All metallic tastes make us think of *syphilis* or of *tubercular* element.)

Important Notes :

Taste should be neutral and any perversion or falsification has a miasmatic basis.

Foul taste of Nux-v. worse morning.

Bitter taste of Bry. worse morning.

Nat-m. and Phos. have a bloody taste.

Elaps. has bloody taste before coughing.

Mercury has a metallic taste.

Hep., Tub. and Pyrog. have taste of pus before coughing.   – Phyllis Speight

DESIRES AND AVERSIONS

– Likes cold foods (R).

(Desires for too hot or too cold is tubercular.)

– Desire for indigestible things, chalk, lime, slate, pencils etc. (Tubercular patients will also crave for such a thing which will be harmful to them and will not be assimilated by their system; this is more in young girls, children and in pregnant women. They are great cravers for peculiar things e.g. salt. They eat more salt than all the family put together. Longs for stimulants, beer, wines or hot aromatic things, craves potatoes and meat.)

– Syphilis patients have aversion to meat. They desire cold things to eat and drink.

CHEST AND LUNGS

– Barking cough, one or two in number.

THE HEART

Very little mental disturbances in heart troubles of a syphilitic and sycotic patients, even at critical periods of the disease. They may have heart troubles for years without causing them any more than occasional dyspnoea or some pain. They die suddenly without warning. The patients usually deny they have any cardiac troubles or they are usually unaware of them (P).

The syphilitic and sycotic heart conditions are much more dangerous than the psoric (R).

BOWELS AND INTESTINAL TRACT

The mercuries represent syphilis in its disease picture.

- The syphilitic or tubercular patients are worse at night; they are driven out of bed by their diarrhoeas, sometimes this is accompanied with profuse warm or cold perspiration, which is very exhausting and debilitating (P).

URINARY ORGANS

- Fibrous changes in kidneys.

SEXUAL SPHERE

- Erections troublesome, painful or without sexual desire.

UPPER AND LOWER EXTREMITIES

Tubercular and syphilitic bone pains are very similar in their character and the time of aggravation (P).

- Stitching, shooting or lancinating pains in the periosteum or long bones of the upper and lower extremities (P).
- Worse at night, or approach of night, worse change of weather, by cold and damp (P).
- *Talipes.* (May be tubercular also.)

–   Nails, show inflammatory changes due to syphilis and
    tuberculosis. Both have true onychia though not of such
    specific character in the tubercular process as in the
    tertiary syphilis.

–   Nails are thin and bend easily, sometimes spoon-shaped.
    (Thin nails with white markings are tubercular.)

–   Paralytic diseases, oedematous swellings, anasarcas may
    be sycotic, syphilitic or tubercular.

SKIN

–   Eruptions around the joints, flexures, arranged in circular
    groupings, ring or segments. Copper coloured or raw ham
    colour, brownish or very red at their base. No itching and
    very little soreness (P).

–   Scales and crusts thick and heavy, patchy and in
    circumscribed spots (P).

–   Skin affection with glandular involvement, will
    necessarily be syphilitic or tubercular (P).

–   Gangrene or gangrenous spots (could be tubercular). In
    dry gangrene, syphilis is always present (P).

–   Condylomata will reveal the presence of both syphilis and
    sycosis, also Verruca acuminate, pointed papillary
    growths, coxcomb and warts (P).

–   In tubercular and syphilitic patients we see much scarring
    and increase in cicatricial tissue.

–   Verruca vulgaris is found in children suffering from
    hereditary syphilis.

–   Verruca filiforms as a tertiary lesion is an indication of
    acquired syphilis.

– The malignancies of syphilis are prone to develop at the age of 40 (P).

Special Notes :

1. Ichthyosis (fish skin) has all the chronic miasms. It is usually incurable, especially if hereditary.

2. In ichthyosis we see the dryness of psora, the squamae of syphilis and often moles and warty eruptions of sycosis.

3. Erysipelas, carcinoma, epithelioma and lupus are multi miasmatic disease.

4. In nevus or congenital markings of the skin we have all the miasms e.g. elephantiasis.

– Phillis Speight

SYPHILITIC MIASM
SUMMARY

1. Syphilis miasm of ancient times and today's pathogen of venereal disease, the Treponema/Spirochaete pallidum are all synonymous.

2. These pathogens mainly create destruction and perversion in the organism. Hence it is called the destructive miasm.

3. Syphilis produces destructive disorders everywhere, mental or physical (J.N.K.).

4. Syphilis mainly develops the virulent open ulcer.

5. We can recognise syphilis by degeneration. It represents an involution which is equivalent to repulsion and destruction of the mind as well as of the organs. There is presence of spasms, ulcers, degeneration of the tissues, burning passions, homicide and wickedness. This miasm corresponds to the red colour of blood and of consuming fire (P.S.O.).

INDICATIONS OF SYPHILITIC MIASMATIC STATES

i)   Destruction/Perversion/Dissolution or Degeneration is the most significant characteristic of syphilis. The patient can very easily destroy himself, or anybody or any precious thing cold-bloodedly. An urge for destruction seems to be his only emotion. All the fascists, anarchists and exploiters of the world are the products of syphilis.

ii) Mentally dull, heavy, stupid, morose and usually suspicious. The intellectual power slowly gets blunted.

   Restless.

   Fixed ideas, fixed in moods.

   Slow in reaction.

   Obstinate.

   Melancholy.

   Depressed. The patient keeps his depression to himself. The first thing you know that he has committed suicide. He is a close mouthed fellow.

   Moral degeneracy, dishonesty.

iii) Syphilis effects most vital organs, like brain; heart, eyes, bone and periosteum.

iv) Ulcer – *Syphilis* has always tendency to develop open ulcer of virulent type. We know that *psora* develops the itch and *sycosis* the catarrhal discharge.

v)   Swelling and inflammation of the glands with a tendency to create ulceration therein.

vi) Hairs and nails are thin in hereditary syphilis. Baldness, especially complete baldness.

vii) Aggravation from natural discharges. Psoric patients are ameliorated from natural discharges, sycotic patients feels no amelioration or aggravation from it.

viii) Putridity or offensiveness from all discharges.

ix) Aggravation at night, from warmth and from sweat and also from natural discharges.

Amelioration in day-time and from cold.

Extreme hot and cold is intolerable.

x) Skin eruptions are full of ulcerations, pains, pus and blood with offensive odour but almost without itching. Copper coloured skin without itching. Gangrene. Scaly eruption.

xi) Desires cold food and drink, alcohol, wine, smoking which are injurious to him. These are the signs of destructions.

Aversion to animal food. It is also to be noted that when the miasm is active in its destructive nature, there is no liking.

xii) Copper or metallic taste in the mouth. We know, burnt taste is psoric. Putrid, musty or fishy taste is *sycotic*.

Taste should be neutral, any perversion has a miasmatic basis.

xiii) A patient with family history of anyone of the following diseases as azoospermia, sterility, abortions, immature deaths or deaths with cerebral or cardiac attack, suicidal deaths, insanity, cancer, tuberculosis, syphilis, etc. are the indication of syphilis.

xiv) The malignancies of syphilis are prone to develop at the age of 40 whereas *Psora,* and *Sycosis* at any age.

xv) Suppressed syphilis flies to the meninges of the brain or the brain itself, larynx, throat, eyes, bones and periosteum.

xvi) Organic changes with degenerative disease such as degeneration of liver, cancer of ulcerative types, tuberculosis, pernicious anaemia, G.P.I. (General Paralysis of the Insane), tabes dorsalis, stricture or stenosis, sinus, fistula, high blood pressure, cerebral or cardiac diseases are the indications of syphilis.

OTHER INDICATIONS :

Syphilis disturbs metabolism of the mineral elements as manifested by dwarfism, anaemia, emaciation, defective formation of bone and teeth and so on.

Syphilis tends to produce deficient growth from brain to bone as it affects the metabolism of the higher elements.

Syphilis prefers the tissues of mesodermal origin.

ANTI-SYPHILITIC REMEDIES

'A' Grade : Ars-i., Aur., Aru-ın-n, Calo., Carc., Kali-i., Kali-s., Lach., Merc-c., Merc-i-f., Merc-i-r., Merc., Nit-ac., Phyt., Sil., Still., Syph., Tub.

'B' Grade : Aethi-m., Ars., Ars-met., Aur-ar., Aur-br., Aur-i., Aur-m., Aur-m-k., Ars-s-f., Calc-ar., Calc-f., Calc-i., Calc-s., Carb.-an., Cinnb., Con., Fl-ac., Guaj., Hep., Iod., Kali-ar., Kali-bi, Kali-c., K-chl., Kali-m., Kreos., Led., Lyc., Med., Merc-aur., Merc-br., Merc-n., Merc-p., Merc-pr-r., Merc-sul., Merc-tn., Merc-v., Merc-p-i., Merc-b-i., Merc-cy., Merc-d., Heater - Syph., Rachi - Syph., Mez., Phos-ac., Phos., Sars., Staph., Sulph., Sulph-i., Thuj.

'C' Grade : Anac., Aur., Arg-cy., Arg-m., Bad., Bapt., Ben-ac., Carb-v., Clem., Cor-r., Cory., Crot-h., Gua., Hecla., Kali-m., Kalm., Osm., Petro., Plat., Plat-m., Rhus-g.

5. CHRONIC MIASM – SYCOSIS

DEVELOPMENT

This miasm pervades internally the human organism and after complete development in the body manifests itself locally by the excrescences. They appear usually, but not always, with a sort of gonorrhoea from the urethra, several days or several weeks, even many weeks (incubation period), after infection through impure coition. More rarely they appear dry and like warts, more frequently soft, spongy, emitting a specifically fetid fluid, bleeding easily, and in the form of a coxcomb or a cauliflower. In males these sprout forth on the glans and on or below the prepuce, but in women, on the parts surrounding the pudenda, and the pudenda itself, which is swollen, are often covered by a great number of them.

Regarding the development of sycosis and sycotic state, it is also to be noted that Dr. J.C. Burnett after prolong and careful observation had noticed that repeated anti-pox vaccination creates such a condition which is very much akin to sycosis (Ref. : His famous book – "Vaccinosis and Its Cure by Thuja"). He called it *Vaccinosis.* Thuja is capable of removing the bad effects of vaccine which is also a great antisycotic remedy. There are other 'A' grade medicines like *Malandrinum, Su., Sulphur* which also antidote the bed effects of this vaccine. In this way number of sycotic patients have become multitudinous in the world of miasms.

SECONDARY MANIFESTATIONS

These sorts of sycotic excrescences were treated by allopaths always in the most violent external way by cauterisation, burning, cutting, or by ligatures. When these are removed in this manner, the natural proximate effects is that they will usually come forth again, subjected again, in vain to a similar, painful, cruel treatment. But even if they could be rooted out in this way, it would merely have the consequence, that the figwart disease, after having been deprived of the local symptoms continues to develop internally and appear in other and much worse ways in secondary ailments.

TREATMENT

A. *Uncomplicated Sycosis*

In such a condition the gonorrhoea dependent on the figwart miasm as well as the whole sycosis is cured most thoroughly through the internal use of a few courses of Thuj. in LM potencies, which in this case is often homoeopathic. This treatment facilitates and strengthens its ability of affecting the living is organism. When their action is exhausted they are to be alterated with Nit-ac. starting from the lowest degrees (i.e. with any degree from LM/1 to LM/3) and to be continued as long as the improvement follows, in order to remove the gonorrhoea and the whole sycosis, i.e. the excrescences. There is no necessity to use any external application.

B. *When Sycosis is complicated with Psora*

If the patient is at the same time affected with another chronic disease, as is common after the violent treatment of figwarts by allopaths, then we often find developed psora complicated with sycosis. In these cases treatment should be followed as under :

(i) Anti-psoric treatment is to be started with well selected anti-psoric medicine on the basis of totality of symptoms. By this the developed psora will go into latent state and sycotic state will be predominant.

(ii) Then the anti-sycotic treatment should be done with the well-selected medicine.

(iii) Afterwards the anti-psoric treatment may be started again.

Hence anti-psoric treatment is to be followed by anti sycotic treatment which is again to be followed by anti-psoric.

In this way, the same alternating treatment may be continued until a complete cure is effected.

C. *When Sycosis complicated with both Developed Psora and Developed Syphilis*

(i) First of all anti-psoric treatment is to be given in the form of well selected anti-psoric medicines.

(ii) It should be followed by anti-sycotic or anti-syphilitic treatment as per the predominance of symptoms.

(iii) Then the remaining one should be treated by proper anti-miasmatic remedies.

(iv) Lastly, this should again be followed by anti-psoric treatment on the basis of the then totality of symptoms.

Thus, the same alternating treatment may be continued, until a homoeopathic cure is effected.

In this dependable cure of sycosis from within through homoeopathy, no external remedy should be applied on the figwarts. Though Hahnemann advises us to apply juice of Thuj. in the moist variety, but according to my last 30 years experiments and experiences I did not find any necessity for the same. Medicinal solution of the well selected medicine in LM degrees which is being taken by the patient may be applied externally also. In this way we can treat the sycosis, the figwarts disease very successfully.

SYMPTOMS OF LATENT SYCOSIS

MIND
- Fixed ideas.
- Suspicious. Restless. Jealous and cruel.
- Loss of memory with regard to recent events, though the events of the long past are well remembered.

HEAD
- Alopecia areata.

NOSE
- Redness of the nose.

JOINTS
- Rheumatic diathesis.

NAILS
- Thick, ridgy and corrugated nails.

FEMALE SEXUAL ORGAN
- Leucorrhoea, smelling like fish brine.

OTHERS
- Anaemia.
- Very slow recovery from acute diseases or the period of convalescence is unusually prolonged.
- Warts, warty growths (condylomata) or moles.

AGGRAVATION & AMELIORATION
- Complaints aggravate in humid atmosphere.
- Walking or light exercise ameliorates. Amelioration by natural discharge which is green or greenish-yellow in colour.
- Intolerance to spices, wine and meat which aggravate all troubles.

SECONDARY MANIFESTATIONS
OF SYCOSIS

MIND

- Cross, irritable and disposed to fits of anger.
- Oppression and anxiety when weather changes.
- Suspicious, the suspicion extends to a point where he dare not trust himself, and he must go back and repeat what he has done or said and wonders if he has said just what he means, he goes back and starts again. He is suspicious that he will be misunderstood, that his hearers will give the wrong meaning to what he is attempting to convey. This suspicion when turned upon others leads to the worst forms of jealousy of his friends, for he knows fully well that he is not understood (R).
- There is a peculiar tendency for making a secret of everything (P).
- If he writes or says something he will repeat it over and over – he always suspects that the idea has not been correctly laid out (P).
- He broods over things (B).
- Sycosis coupled with psora is the basis of criminal insanity and of most suicides (R).
- Men and women who commit suicide today are mainly sycotic (P).
- Sorrowful.
- When syphilis and sycosis are combined, these patients are sullen, smouldering, threating to break out into dangerous manifestations (R).

- Degenerations are sycotic or syphilitic or result from both (R).
- The sycotic taint develops the worst forms of degeneracy, because of the basic suspicion and jealousy, patients will resort to any and all means of vindicating themselves in their own light. The most marked degeneration of the stigmata is its suspicions, its quarrelsomeness, tendency to harm others and to harm animals. This produces the worst forms of cruelty and cunning deceit and the worst forms of mania of any of the stigmata (R).
- Sycosis is the most mischievous of all the miasms. He is ever bent upon the mischieves and misdeeds. The sycotic mind is so grossly debased that it makes the victim devoid of all sense of righteousness. It a liar, a vicious scoundrel, destitute of all love and affection for others, makes him mean and selfish. *All the vicious individuals on earth – thieves, robbers and murderers, are the products of sycosis. It makes a beast out of man (B).*
- Absent-minded only in certain things. Forgets words, sentences and previous lines that he just read – he wanders how the simplest words are spelled; he has momentary loss of thought or he loses the thread of his discourse frequently; he is constantly stopping to find it, which causes him to repeat. Often this is due to his inability to find the right word. During writing, he is not certain of using the right words or he is in doubt about spelling. He drops words or letters or uses wrong ones (P).
- Absent-minded (P.S.O.).
- Has difficulty in giving his case to the physician – he is afraid he will not give it correctly. While speaking, is

afraid that he will forget something. This is painful to him and cause him much annoyance and suffering (P).

- Reading and any mental effort – causes pain in head (P).

- Recollection of recent events difficult while they can recall things of the past.

- In both the sycosis and syphilis, the reasoning powers are slow and they are constantly condemning self.

- In cases of both venereal miasms these patients are better off their mental stress and disturbances, like psora, by some external expression of the disease; for instance, return of a leucorrhoeal, gonorrhoeal or catarrhal discharge of any form ameliorates a sycotic patient at once.

- In the tertiary stage of sycosis patient is better by an eruption of warts (P). Mental conditions of sycotic are all better when warts of fibrous growth appear; they are always better in general from return of open ulcers or old sores and markedly by return of acute gonorrhoeal manifestation (R).

- Self condemnation is the moral reaction to the inception of the diseased state (R).

- To sum up, the mentality of sycosis is suspicious, mischievous, mean, selfish and forgetful (B).

[The mental symptoms arising from moral insanity usually arise from mixed miasm and Sycosis combined with Psora figures largely in the criminality of our country (P).]

SENSORIUM

- Vertigo beginning in the base of the brain is more apt to be of a sycotic or syphilitic nature or may be of tubercular origin.

- Vertigo on closing eyes, disappearing on opening eyes.

- Sensation as if the continuity of the body will be dissolved, as if the whole body were thin or extremely delicate and would not resist the least attack or touch or even approach (J.N.K.). As if insects were on the occiput or temples or as if a living animal were moving inside the abdomen, as if the testes were moving, as if drops were falling on the chest and so on (J.N.K.).

HEAD

- Headache – frontal or on vertex, worse at or after midnight.

- Headaches of sycotic children are more common than we think, worse at night, producing feverishness, restlessness, crying, fretting, and worrying. Better by motion. Headache in vertex or there may be a frontal headache; these are worse by lying down and at night, especially after midnight (R).

- The patient is restless and wants to be kept in motion which ameliorates (R).

- Head symptoms resembles the syphilitic, in having the night aggravation and there is the same type of vertigo at the base of brain (R).

- Headaches worse on lying down and at night (P).

- Headaches usually worse riding, better by motion, worse by exertion either mental or physical (P).

- Usually accompanied by coldness of body, sadness and prostration (R).

OUTER HEAD

- Hair falls out in little circular patches.

- Fishy odour from hair.

- Child smells sour.

- Stubby, dead, broken hair in beard.

SCALP

- The hair falls out in circular spots; the hair of the beard falls (R).

- The sycotic scalp perspires but there are no moist matting eruptions of syphilis (R).

EYES AND VISION

- Ulceration and specific inflammation, corneal inflammation in young people. Chronic corneal ulcers in children where there is no trace of syphilis but based on tubercular diathesis. Sycosis never gives a true ulcer (P).

   [Thick copious pus formation or discharges, especially if greenish or yellowish-green are distinctly tubercular or syphilitic (P).]

- Gout of the eyes.

- Arthritic troubles of the eyes are a combination of *sycosis and psora;* there are also neuralgias which are worse in rainy weather (R).

- Sycotic pains may come on at any time but are worse by barometer changes or by moisture, rainy or stormy weather.

- Babies born of sycotic parents sometimes have ophthalmia neonatorum.

EAR

–   Gouty concretion in ears of baby born of sycotic parents.

NOSE AND SMELL

–   Loss of smell.

–   Hay fever – nose clear one hour, the next moment nasal passages are blocked.

–   Red nose with enlarged capillaries.

–   Snuffles in children. No ulceration and no crusts, if purulent, very scanty and has the odour of fish brine or stale fish.

–   Stoppage is due to local congestion and thickening of the membrane or enlargement of the turbinated bodies due to congestion, the discharge is yellowish-green, scanty except in fresh winds when it is copious thin mucus.

–   New babies of sycotic parents often get "snuffles" – nose dry, stuffed up; frequently child will scream with anger in its attempt to breathe with its mouth closed. May last few days or weeks but usually displaced by something more serious, especially if local measures are applied to relieve it.

–   Children from sycotic parents complicated with gout take cold easily at slightest exposure and frequently suffer from acute coryza – discharge from nose become copious, watery and often excoriating.

–   Gouty concretion in nose (P).

FACE

–   Erysipelas of face, psoric and sycotic.

–   All warty eruption, moles, papilomats (P).

MOUTH

– Gouty concretions in mouth of young baby, born of sycotic parents (P).

TASTE

– A putrid, musty or fishy taste (P).

DESIRES – AVERSIONS

– Craves beer though this is not a desirable element in his diet, but it causes much less aggravation than to wines (P).

– Meats arouse the latent sycosis as in psora.

The sycotic patient should take sparingly of meat and should have more nuts, beans or cheese. Gouty patients cannot digest nuts (R).

– Likes either hot or cold foods (I').

STOMACH

– Patients, especially children are worse by eating any kind of food whatever and are better by lying on stomach or by pressure over region of stomach, by violent motion, walking, rocking, etc. Pains are always crampy or colicky, paroxysmal, and better by hard pressure and motion (p).

– Meat in sycotics stimulates or assists in developing the uric acid and gouty diathesis (P).

– Prefer beer, rich and fat meats – well seasoned with salt and pepper (P).

– They are better from hot drinks and prefer food warm.

– Children born of sycotic parents often suffer from colic almost from the moment of births; not the ordinary flatulent colic but one of severe and specific nature continuing often from one to three months after birth. The sufferings that these children have to undergo are simply indescribable; they writhe and twist and squirm with pain, drawing up their limbs and screaming often for hours at a time. The pain usually comes in paroxysms or it is better by pressure or by the child lying on the stomach or by being carried about; shaking or rocking gently seems to pacify things. Heat gives temporary relief but all food worsen greatly, even the mother's milk, although food when first taken seems to ameliorate for some time. Gas is frequently expelled from the stomach with great force and is often quite pathogno-monic, of sycotic colic. Many times relief has been given with *Lyc.* or *Argentum nitricum,* both remedies seem frequently required.

CHEST-LUNGS

– Cough of sycosis has very little expectoration, usually of clear mucus; occasionally this is ropy and may also be of cottony nature. A great deal of coughing is required to take it out, hence the prolonged teasing cough.

– Coughs of sycotics are usually bronchial. Always having bronchitis, hard, dry, racking coughs, often in early autumn and/or winter. Often the troubles begin with coryza – much sneezing with profuse watery flow from nose – in a few days it will go down to the bronchi and they have a week, ten days or longer duration of coughing spells. Expectoration scanty. In summer usually free but always taking cold in the head on least exposure to cold air or dampness. They cannot as a rule breathe through the nose (P).

– Imperfect oxidation of food products and their deposits in tissues in the form of gouty concretions and lithic formations (P).

HEART

– Violent hammering and beating about the heart due to reflexes, such as gastric disturbances, flatulence and uterine irritation, especially if local applications are used to relieve the pain (P).

– Heart patient is better by motion like walking, riding or gentle exercise (P).

– Fluttering, oppression and difficult breathing at intervals. Seldom much pain or suffering unless in rheumatic difficulties. We may find severly painful rheumatism, but not so constant or persistent as psoric. Much soreness and tenderness, often worse by motion of arms. Pain from shoulder to heart, or from heart to scapula in rheumatic cardiac troubles (P).

– Often pulse is soft, slow and easily comprehensible.

– Valves become roughened due to acidic condition of system, the walls enlarged, the muscles flabby, soft and lacking power. Patients as a rule are fleshy and puffy, their obesity often lies at the bottom of their dyspnoea, and they are constantly gaining flesh. (P).

– Frequent blue face, synovitis and apt to have venous congestion or rather stagnation. These conditions are very much worse for high living, rich spicy food or spirituous liquor. (R).

– Gout of the heart.

- Combination of sycosis and psora are the right soil for valvular and cardiac disturbances with changes in organ structure. These are the conditions that cause the fatalities. In patients with sycotic heart conditions there is fear and apprehension that we find in psoric patients. (R).

ABDOMEN

- Sycotic colic is betterly doubling up, motion or hard pressure. True colic – colicky pains in bowel troubles of children. Often the simplest form of food produces colic and pain in abdomen or throughout the intestinal tract (P).

- Ulceration of umbilicus in a sycotic child with the tubercular element, having the yellowish-green, watery, thin, excoriating and offensive pus, often of a fishy or fish brine odour. (P).

BOWELS AND INTESTINAL TRACT

- Colic rather than diarrhoea but if the latter it is spasmodic and of a colicky nature, accompanied with a slimy, mucous stool and griping colic and rectal tenesmus. Stools of *Rheum, Cham.* and *Mag-c.* are typical. (P). These diarrhoeas have the most pain and stools are forcibly ejected from the rectum. *Crot-t., Cham., Coloc., Laur.,* etc., are indicative (P).

- Intestinal pains – colicky and makes the patient angry. All bowel trouble produce irritability. They are cross and irritable with their pains; stools are changeable, usually greenish-yellow mucus, seldom bloody; greenish, watery, sour-smelling with cutting colic – even the child smells sour in marked cases of inherited sycosis (P).

F - 7

- Sycotic children want to be rocked constantly or carried or moved about. The colics are better by firm pressure or lying on abdomen, they are worse eating fruit (P).

    (Dulcamara has a typical sycotic stool. Diarrhoea from getting wet.)

- The grass green stool of Ip., Mag-c., Crot-t., Grat., Arg-n., etc., are apt to be sycotic. (P).

- Bleeding haemorrhoids.

- Pruritis, scanty, thin, watery discharge oozing from rectum, that has fishy or fish-brine odor.

- Stricture in the rectum, sinuses, fistulae and fistulous pockets are all of a tubercular origin but are greatly manifested by sycosis.

- Cancerous affections, malignant growths, and such diseases are multi-miasmatic, especially the sycotic and the tubercular combined. Psora can never be left out of malignancies no matter what other elements may combine with it; it fathers them all. (P).

- Rectum – when there is an addition of the sycotic stigma the conditions are greatly aggravated, and there is much more tendency towards malignancy, for combinations of the tubercular diathesis with sycosis produce cancerous affections (R).

URINARY ORGANS

- Sycotic children scream, when urinating, (Lyc., Sars.).

- Painful spasms affecting urethra and bladder.

- Gout of the bladder. Gouty concretions in urethra of young babies who have sycotic parents.

- If sycosis is present in these diabetic patients it is more malignant and more fatal.
- Bright's disease.
- Fibrous changes in kidneys.
- Prostatic troubles where sycosis is the exciting medium.

SEXUAL ORGANS

- Pains and diseases of uterus and reproductive organs are spasmodic, colicky, and often paroxysmal – acrid discharges, pruritis, painful and often frequent urination, fish-brine or stale fish odour of catarrhal discharges.

    (The menstrual pains of Sycosis can well be understood when we study remedies such as *Colo., Mag-c., Croc., Sep., Lac-c., Caul.)* Another class that represents the rheumatic element are *Rhus-t., Bry., Cham., Colch., Lyco., Dulc., Phyto., Puls.,* etc.

- Menstrual flow acrid, excoriating, biting and burning the pudendum.

- Menstrual pains are spasmodic, extremely sharp, colicky, coming in paroxysms – the flow often only with the pain, offensive, clotted, stringy, large, dark, even black. Usually excoriating and acrid.

- Leucorrhoea thin, looks like dirty green water, sometimes greenish-yellow, scanty, acrid, producing biting or itching and burning of parts. Odour of stale fish or fish-brine. May be pungent or like that of decayed fish. Patient forever taking douches on account of odour and acridity or discharge. Often this produces little vesicles of excoriations on the pudendum which are a source of great annoyance to patient.

– Many of the ovarian or tubercular symptoms that develop during menses are dependent more on Sycosis than any other miasm.

– The most frequent location of the sycotic manifestation in woman is in the pelvic organs. Pelvic inflammations such as an inflammation of the ovaries, inflammation processes of the fallopian tubes, in fact all pelvic inflammatory disease (PID) may be traced to this taint. In more chronic types we get cystic degeneration of the ovaries, the uterus and the fallopian tubes.

– Again the infection may pass on into the peritoneal cavity hence peritonitis and general cellulitis.

– Appendicitis is directly traceable to sycotic influences (R).

– The fish-brine odour is characteristic of the sycotic taint, which may appear in all discharges but especially in the discharges of the genital tract (R).

– Frequent and/or strong erections.

EXTREMITIES

– Pains in joints or periosteum are due to gouty concretions or chalky deposits in the tissues conveyed from circulation.

– Shooting or tearing pains in the muscles or joints. Pains in fingers or small joints. Worse rest, patients is better moving, by rubbing, stretching and better in dry, fair weather; worse at approach of storm or a damp, humid atmosphere, and a falling barometer, or becoming cold; heat does not always ameliorate.

– Stiffness and soreness, especially lameness, is very characteristic of sycosis. Worse stooping, bending or beginning to move.

- In arthritis or rheumatism we have an infiltration of inflammatory deposits but gets readily absorbed and is never formative as we find in syphilitic and tubercular changes which are permanent unless dissipated by treatment (P).
- Rheumatic pains worse during cold damp, better moving or stretching (R).
- Arthritic - deformans - sycotic (R).
- Nails ridged or ribbed.
- Chilblains is a multi miasmatic dis – there is the tubercular taint, with a sycotic element as a base – that is why they prove such a dreadful disease producing agent when suppressed by local measures (P).
- Paralytic disease, oedematous swellings, anasarca and such are sycotic, syphilitic and tubercular (P).
- Gout : Gouty diathesis, rheumatic gout (P).

SKIN
- Scales patchy and in circumscribed spots.
- Eczema – exfoliate.
- Circinatus herpes and herpes zoster.
- Lichen – sycosis and tubercular.
- Tinea barbae. Tinea tonsuraus.
- Tinea vesicular.
- Wart and warty growths.
- Condylomata will reveal the presence of both syphilis and sycosis, also verruca acuminate, pointed papillary growths, coxcomb and warts (P).

- Skin lesions in tertiary stage, warty eruptions or growths – verruca filiformis, verruca vulgaris, verruca plana.

- Verruca plana is another hereditary form, found more or less upon the backs of hands and faces of children and young people.

- The filiformis appears in adults with acquired sycosis who have had it suppressed. Usually appear on sexual organs, trunk of body—small in diameter, one-eighth of an inch long, often shorter, brownish or greyish, pointed with spindle like attachments (P).

- Acne – large red, angry, blunt pointed looking papules at about menstrual period ; they do not suppurate, but are sore to touch and sensitive – quite isolated and separate from each other.

- Lupus – whether of erythematous or of the common form, belongs without doubt to the tubercular family of skin diseases with a sycotic element (P).

- The malignancies develop at any age.

- Malignancies of the skin are more violent and intractable in proportion as the sycotic taint is increased (P).

- All forms of facial skin diseases that are contracted in barber's shop except Tinea favusa (P).

- In scalp and beard Tinea circumscripta which causes a form of alopecia..

- All forms of ringworm. The suppression of ringworm brings rheumatism, chronic headaches, stomach troubles, chronic bronchitis, chronic coughs, melancholia, mania, hysteria in women and malignancies. Variola and varicella in all their different forms have very marked characteristics of the sycotic element present, or of syphilis and sycosis combined (P).

– The serum of vaccination has both of these elements present.

– Erythematous eczema; erysipelas, especially in the phlegmonous variety; herpes zoster and impetigo contagiosa.

– Psoriasis has the gouty element so characteristic of sycosis.

– The spider dot (tertiary) upper portion of face usually about half an inch below the lower eyelid or over centre of malar bone consists of little sprangle of dilated capillaries, resembling somewhat the meshes of the spider's web. In children – pale or bleached or quite red and prominent. Red mole – a tertiary symptom, pinhead to pea–smooth, round, shiny, often red as blood, appearance of polka dot on skin. Condylomata.

– If sycotic element is present, in abdominal operations, the possibility of a stitch abscess is increased (P).

Dr. Phyllis Speight's Additional Notes on Sycosis

The sycotic patient is a barometer. When it rains he has pain; when the atmosphere is filled with moisture he suffers; when the elements clash, his organism is at war with itself; the rain, the snow, the cold, the barometre's rise and fall, are his enemies.

Sycosis, if present in any form or in any stage, usually taken the precedence of the three miasms.

Sycosis, while there is a much amelioration by eliminative processes, natural elimination such as diarrhoea, free urination or even perspiration does not ameliorate (R).

Sycotic manifestations are characterised by slowness of recovery.

Sycosis develops the catarrhal discharge.

SYCOTIC MIASM
SUMMARY

1. Sycotic miasm of ancient period and pathogen of one of venereal disease of today, the gonococcus are all synonymous.

2. This pathogen mainly produces incoordination or proliferation in the organism. Hence it is called the incoordinating miasm.

    Sycosis produces incoordination everywhere, mental or physical; the latter by uncontrolled proliferation and/or atrophy of different parts of tissues (J.N.K.).

3. Sycosis develops the catarrhal discharge.

4. We recognise sycosis, characterized by ostentation; its hastiness, its tendency to externalize and exaggerate, its abnormal increase in the frequency. The dimensions, and in the intensity of the sickness, as in the concomitant instability. Everything which tends to exaggerate the expression of self-hyperfunction, hypertrophy, etc., is part of this yellowest of miasms (P.S.O.).

INDICATIONS OF SYCOTIC
MIASMATIC STATES

i) Inco-ordination, intemperance, excess, or a proliferation of tissues is the most significant indication of sycosis.

ii) Mentally suspicious. Develops the worst forms of degeneracy, because of the basic suspicion and jealousy, privacy. Tendency for making a secret of everything. Strict privacy, concealment.

Sycosis broods over things (B).

Sycosis coupled with psora is the basis of criminal insanity and of most suicides. (R). Men and women who commit suicide today are mainly sycotic (P).

Sycosis is the most mischievous of all the miasms. He is ever bent upon the mischiefs and misdeeds. Sycotic mind is grossly debased. Sycosis makes the victims devoid of all sense of righteousness. It makes him a liar, vicious scoundrel, destitute of all love and affection for others, mean and selfish. All the vicious individuals on earth – thieves, robbers and murderers are the products of sycosis. It makes a beast out of man (B).

Forgetful. Recollection of recent events difficult, whilst they can recall things of the past (P).

Absent minded.

Fixed ideas. Blind faith in imaginary matters or loss of religious devotion.

Cross.

Irritable.

Fear. Despair, despair of recovery, dissatisfaction, repentance.

To sum up, the mentality of Sycosis is suspicion, mischievous, mean, selfish and forgetful (B).

Sensation as if the continuity of the body will be dissolved, as if living animals were moving inside the body.

iii) Joints and connective tissues are affected.

iv) Sycosis develops the catarrhal discharge as we all know, psora the itch and syphilis the open ulcer.

v) Condylomatous growth.

Warts. Moles.

Unusual fleshy growths, all kinds of tumours and tumorous growth.

Excrescences. Malformation. For that reason it is also called formative miasm.

Hyperthyroidism.

Talipes or clubfoot, etc.

Barber's rash.

Eczema, ring-worms, with cracks and sticky fluids oozes.

Skin oily.

Haemangioma.

Anosmia.

vi) Acquired gonorrhoea or history of hereditary gonorrhoea.

vii) Hairs are thick and coarse. Small bald patches on head and face. Unwanted hair.

Nails ridged or ribbed. Nails are thick.

Thin and spotted nails, or white specks on the nails are indications of tubercular miasm.

viii) Slow recovery, even acute disease recovers very slowly.

ix) Asthma, history of asthma, bronchial asthma or gonorrhoea.

x) Chronic or long continued inflammation, specially of joints.

xi) Inflammation or blockage of fallopian tube and sterility due to that uterine tumour.

xii) Sudden onset of any severe disease.

xiii) Oedema or anasarca in any part or of the whole organism.

xiv) Enlargement of prostate gland. Appendicitis. Anaemia.

xv) Worse from rest, rain and rainy season, damp cold weather and places, 4 to 6 a.m., mid-day to midnight, cold. Pain when rains is one of the great indications of sycosis; when the humidity is high.

Better by movement, while in active condition, heat (P).

Natural parasympathetic functioning like diarrhoea, free urination, even perspiration, gives no amelioration (or aggravats – Author) to any of its conditions (J.N.K.).

xvi) Malignancies of sycosis are prone to develop at any age.

xvii) If suppressed sycosis attacks the internal organs, especially the pelvic and sexual organs produces inflammation hypertrophies, abscesses, cystic degeneration, mucous cysts, etc., and when thrown up the brain it produces headaches, severe acute mania, central insanity, moral degeneracy, dishonesty, etc.

xviii)Sycosis disturbs general metabolism and is manifested by dwarfism, emaciation of particular parts, anaemia, cretinism, myxedema and Addison's disease.

Sycosis tends to produce deficient growth from brain to bone hence inducing incoordination of the whole metabolism.

Sycosis prefers the tissues of exodermal origin.

ANTI-SYCOTIC REMEDIES

A. Grade : Arg-met., Arg-n., Kali-s., Medo., Mur-ac., Nat-m., Nat-s., Nit-ac., Sep., Staph., Thuj.

B. **Grade** : Agar., Apis., Ars., Ast-r., Aur-m., Bar-c., Calc-ar., Calc., Caust., Dulc., Ferr-m., Fl-ac., Graph., Iod., Kali-ar., Kali-bi., Kali-m., Lach, Lyc., Mang-m., Mez., Phos., Phyt., Plat., Psor., Pyro., Sars., Sec-c., Sel., Sil., Sulph.

C Grade : Alumn., Alum., Anac., Ant-c., Ant-t. Aran., Aur-m., Bry., Carb-an., Carb-s., Carb-v., Cham., Cinnb., Con., Euph., Hep., Kali-c., Merc., Petr., Puls., Sabin.

6. NEW MIASMS

In homoeopathic literature there is another miasm which has been designated as 'Pseudo - Psora'. It is also stated that this is the by-product of mixed miasm. We know that mycobacterium or tubercle bacilli had been invented and isolated by Robert Koch in the year 1882. As there cannot be any psora without psoric pathogen – itch mite, syphilis without syphilitic pathogen – Treponema pallidum and sycosis miasm without sycotic pathogen – gonococcus, so there cannot be any tuberculosis without tubercular pathogen-tubercle bacilli. Hence we can no longer define Tuberculosis as the resultant effects of mixed miasm. It should be treated as a separate miasm. This tubercular miasm has also got its distinct characteristics. Some of which I have stated in the chapter- Indications of Syphilitic State. We are also getting 'Mycobacterium Lepra' for Leprosy. Accordingly we can also think about cancer, AIDS in future, if not now. AIDS virus has already been isolated, although causative factor of cancer is yet to be explored. Separate chapters have been given on Tubercular, Cancer and AIDS miasms. The number of venereal miasms are now three instead of two including AIDS. In this way aetiology of chronic diseases and their peculiar indications may be developed gradually. This will assist us in diagnosis, prognosis, management of diseases on one hand and selection of medicine on the other.

SHORT SUMMARY

1. Miasms of ancient period and bacteria and viruses of modern times are synonymous.

2. Only pathogens can not produce diseases. Their toxins are liable for production of diseases.

3. Without favourable condition and susceptibility pathogens and their toxin cannot produce any disease.

4. Pathogens are not only the cause of diseases but the proximate cause. Chronic miasms (pathogens) are the primary reason and that is why some cases continue to relapse despite good therapy.

5.(a) Miasmatic predisposition is not merely a matter involving DNA, since disease acquired during life can transit their influences to subsequent generations (G.V.).

5.(b) Other method of treatment can kill pathogen but cannot remove their toxic effects, so they cannot cure any chronic disease. Only homoeopathy can cure disease as it can remove the toxins and their effects individually and even genetically.

6. The number of miasms will be increased gradually.

7. Tuberculosis, AIDS and cancer may be treated as separate miasms.

8. It is the pathogen (miasms) which create the miasmatic (pathogenic) state, or condition, or diathesis. It is not the diathesis that produces miasms.

9. A miasm is characterised by transmission from generation to generation, and by relief from the corresponding nosode.

10. The predisposition of a child is a combination of the predispositions of the parents. The predisposition transmitted by the parents is a result both of the general state of health and of the specific state

7. CHRONIC MIASM – TUBERCULOSIS

DEVELOPMENT

The specific pathogenic acid-fast organism, namely Mycobacterium tuberculosis is responsible for the production of tuberculosis. In human, Mycobacterium hominies and bovis both play the same important role for establishing the disease. Besides, tuberculosis in bird, fish and vole – Avian type, cold-blooded type and Murine type, respectively in the domain of Mycobacterium tuberculosis are responsible. The name Mycobacterium is taken into consideration due to presence of Mycolic acid and the organisms show branching. As chemical composition of Mycobacterium tuberculosis it contains (a) Mycol – responsible for acid-fast staining, (b) Lipoid-Glyceroid, phosphatides and wax, (c) Poly-saccharide – responsible for necrosis, caseation and tubercle formation and (d) Protein – responsible for immunity and allergy. Hence, tuberculosis may be defined as an acute or chronic communicable disease caused by Mycobacterium tuberculosis and characterised by inflammatory infiltration, tubercle formation, caseation, fibrosis and calcification. In any case, formation of tubercle which is a small rounded nodule in the tissue is the main feature. Microscopically, it has a central area of necrosis and surrounded by nodular collection of epithelioid cells with scattered Langhan's type of giant cells. A zone of lymphocytes is present around the epithelioid cells. The zone of lymphocytes is surrounded by a zone of fibrous tissue and the granulation tissue.

Fransiscus (1614-1672) investigated the pathogenic lesion made by the tubercle bacillus and identified the 'Tubercle'. After that Gaspard Laurent Bayle (1774-1816) named the disease as "Tuberculosis".

In 1882, a German physician, Robert Koch published his classical investigations on tuberculosis and it was proved that tubercle bacillus is the causative agent of tuberculosis. He named this organism as the tubercle bacillus. From his time the word tuberculosis came into general use instead of phthisis. This genus has got both pathogenic and saprophytic (non-pathogenic) species.

Tuberculosis differs in its effects on patients meeting the disease for the first time and in those who already have some resistance due to previous encounter with the organism. The primary tuberculosis occurs mainly in children and young adults and may spread *via* the blood stream to produce the disease at a distance from the initial lesion; the meninges, bones and the genito-urinary tract may all be involved in this way. Most primary tuberculosis is usually a more circumscribed lesion which may extend by necrosis, ulceration and cavitation to give extensive lesions. In the elderly and debilitated people the resistance to the tubercle bacilli may be lost and miliary spread in the blood-stream may occur.

Sites of Infection

1. Lungs.
2. Serous membrane, e.g. pleura, peritonium, pericardium, meninges, etc.
3. Lymph glands, e.g. involvement of regional lymph glands such as cervical, bracheo-bronchial and mesenteric glands.

4. Organs, e.g., intestines, larynx, liver, kidney, spleen, brain, etc.

5. Bones and joints.

6. Fibrous tissues and muscles; of course they are very rarely affected.

7. Generalised tubercles usually known as acute, Miliary tuberculosis.

8. In adults, lungs are the commonest sites of the disease, whereas, in children glands, bones, joints are also usually affected.

Characteristics in progress of Tuberculosis

1. In pulmonary tuberculosis : Fatigue, loss of weight, anorexia, morning and evening rise of temperature, weakness and malaise. Productive cough, haemoptysis, dyspnoea and chest pain is aggravated by respiratory effort.

2. In gastro-intestinal tract : Ulceration, perforation or obstruction with the above general phenomena.

3. In other organs : Destructive changes and symptoms associated with loss of their function.

Characteristics in healing of Tuberculosis

Healing of tuberculosis lesion may take place at any stage by resolution, fibrosis and calcification.

Sources of infection of Tuberculosis

Foetus gets infected transplacentally.

From bad environment, newborn babies are infected.

Both the infants and adults become victims by infested cow's milk, bad environment and bad effect of civilization; bad habit, like – spitting in public places, coughing, sneezing by an infected person, handling of T.B patients unhygienically, the use of utensils of an infected person, such as soiled cups, sauces, spoons, glass, etc., with the long continuous exposure to the above exciting causes, increase the probability to infection of any healthy person.

Entry of Mycobacterium tuberculosis in human body

In pulmonary tuberculosis droplet infection is the first and foremost cause of infection and apex of right lung is the commonest site of infection. Infection process has 3 stages :

(i) Stage of primary complex – area of broncho-pneumonic patch in the lung, lymphangitis and gland involvement.

(ii) Stage of haematogenous dissemination.

(iii) Stage of isolated bronchogenic tuberculosis.

In gastrointestinal tuberculosis, tubercle bacilli take entry into the alimentary tract through mouth and naso-pharynx, get absorbed through intestinal mucosa and enters into the lymph channel and blood, causing enlargement of cervical glands and peyer's patches of small intestine and then pass to mesenteric glands.

Infected cow's milk is the commonest example of this type of infection.

In skin, tubercle bacilli take entry through the minute abrasions in the skin and in primary stage it takes place in the form of lumps vulgaris and verruca tuberculosis.

So, the spreading of disease takes place through three routes:

(a) directly through continuous surface,

(b) through lymph stream and

(c) through blood stream.

Clinical diagnosis of Mycobacterium tuberculosis

1. *Indirect Method*

    This method consists of *allergic reaction (Mantoux test);* complement fixation test; increase in sedimentation of blood corpuscles (E.S.R.); laevodeviation of *Arneth* index.

2. *Direct Method*

    It consists of :

    (a) Culture of sputum in some specific medium, e.g., Dorset's egg medium, *Lowenstein-Jensen's* medium, etc.

    (b) Animal pathogenicity test : Specific concentrated materials are inoculated in animal species mainly rabbit and guineapig. After death of those species within specific date (3 to 9 months in case of human type and 12 weeks in case of bovine type), lungs, kidney, spleen, liver are examined to see whether those organs are affected.

    (c) *Microscopical Examination :* After staining the smear (Ziehl-Neelsen stain) prepared with mucopurulent material from infected person, is examined under microscope to detect bacteria. Besides this, two other methods based on same principle, i.e., concentration technique having individual preparation are employed in the examination under microscope.

These two methods are *Petroff's method* and *Antiformin method.*

Principle, Interpretation and use of Mantoux test.

Old tuberculin prepared from human or bovine stain of Mycobacterium tuberculosis is used as a diagnostic agent for tuberculosis. A person showing a specific sensitivity to tuberculin is considered to have been infected with the tubercle bacillus, although the infection may be inactive.

Sensitivity tests to tuberculin can be performed in different ways. The intracutaneous test of Mantoux gives the most precious results. The diagnostic dose varies with the circumstances because of the great variation in sensitivity to tuberculin.

In a full-scale test, the initial dose injected is I unit of old tuberculin or tuberculin purified protein derivative in 0.1 ml. The point of injection is marked with ink about 5 mm. diameter and area of erythema and induration will be recorded after 48,72 & 96 hours. A positive reaction is characterized by palpable infiltration area which on having the diameter more than 5mm i.e., 5-10mm is indicated by one plus (+), 10-20 mm by two plus (++) and over 20 mm by three plus (+++).

If the reaction is negative, the test is repeated with 10 units in 0.1 ml. and if still negative, the test is also repeated with 100 units in 0.1 ml. before declaring the patient "Mantoux - negative".

In conclusion of the discussion regarding this test, according to so-called modern medicine, it is suggested that if the reaction is positive *in infants,* it has more diagnostic value for tuberculosis, B.C.G. vaccination is contra-indicated here. If the reaction is negative B.C.G. vaccination is indicated. In adults, the positive reaction only indicates present or past lesion.

Though, negative reaction indicates absence of tuberculosis lesion but the reaction becomes negative due to presence of allergy in some acute diseases like small pox, measles, acute miliary tuberculosis. Epidemic and endemic area can also be identified with this test.

TREATMENT OF ORTHODOX SCHOOL

Chemotherapy for a period about 1 year with two or three drugs namely streptomycin, aminosalicylic acid and isoniazide are suggested for the treatment. Now, as standard treatment with isoniazide, refampicin and usually ethambutol as third drug and continue with an appropriate pair of drugs when sensitivities are known.

Drugs used in the treatment of tuberculosis include capreamycin sulphate, cycloserine, ethambutol, ethionamide isoniazide, prothionamide, pyrazinamide, rifampicin, sodium aminosalicylate, streptomycin, thiaceazone and viomycin.

THE SECONDARY SYMPTOMS
OF TUBERCULOSIS

MIND

- Child with union of the syphilitic and psoric dyscrasias presents a picture of "the problem child" – slow in comprehensions, dull, unable to keep a line of thought, unsocial – keeps to himself and becomes sullen and morose (R).
- Temporary amelioration by offensive foot or axillary sweat – which, when suppressed often induces lung trouble or some other severe diseases.
- Mental symptoms are better by an outbreak of an ulcer.
- The epilepsy of psora or the true insanity of psora is usually of a tubercular nature.

SESORIUM

- Vertigo beginning in the base of the brain are more apt to be of a sycotic or syphilitic nature or may be of tubercular origin.

HEAD

- Headaches occurring every Sunday or on rest days, worse riding in carriage, or are due to the least unusual ordeals, as preparing for examination; meeting with strangers and entertaining them. Headaches with deathly coldness of hands and feet, with prostration, sadness and general despondency.
- Headaches with red face and rush of blood to head, or at certain hours of the day, usually in the forenoon.

- Headache better nose-bleed – in fact, anything better by epistaxis is tubercular. Amelioration by rest, sleep & eating.
- Prosopalgia or persistent headache not easily ameliorated by treatment.
- Tubercular (or syphilitic) headache will often last for days and is very severe, often unendurable, sometimes with sensation of bands about the head.
- In the tubercular (or syphilitic) headaches of children, they strike, knock or pound their heads with their hands or against some object.

OUTER HEAD

- Hair dry like tow, dead, like hemp from old rope.
- Hair moist, glues together.
- Offensive odour from head, musty smell like old hay.
- Hair very oily and greasy; moist eruptions on scalp.
- Severe itching of scalp with moist, offensive, matted hair.
- Fetid, sour, oily (child).
- Imperfect, crooked, bent, curved or broken eyelashes.

THE SCALP

- Pustular eruptions with thick yellowish pus.
- Offensive discharges from behind and about the ears.
- Cracks about the ear.
- Moist eczematous eruptions about scalp, with copious pus formation.
- Scalp is moist, perspiring copiously (children).

- Head large, bulging, often open sutures, bones soft, cartilaginous (Children).
- A thick, yellow, heavy crust is apt to be tubercular or syphilitic in origin.
- Heat of head worse at night.
- Aversion to have head uncovered.

EYES AND VISION

- Astigmatism and other marked refractory changes due to malformation. Changes in the lens, sclera, choroid, ciliary body and iris. Processes that change organs and give us perversions of form, shape and size (these are also syphilitic).
- Photophobia much more marked in tuberculosis and syphilis. Dreads artificial light more than sunlight.
- Disturbances in the glandular structures or in the lachrymal apparatus (also in syphilis). Pustular diseases as found in many cases of glandular lids.
- Ulcerations and specific inflammation; ciliary blepharitis, acute or chronic (also in syphilis), scaly, red lids, angry looking.
- Thick, copious pus formation or discharges, especially if greenish or yellowish-green, are distinctly tubercular or sycotic.
- Ciliary neuralgia.
- Arthritic or rheumatic eye troubles are worse by light or after sunset and generally better from hot applications.
- Styes on eyes.

– A chronic dilation of the pupil in children or women. When these patients are affected with exanthematous fevers of any form there is a strong tendency to inflammatory stasis of the eye, and serious eye troubles are apt to follow.

EAR : HEARING

– All organic ear troubles, like suppurative processes and destruction of the ossicles of the ears.

– Ear is often a safety valve in tubercular children. Abscesses relieve quite severe meningeal difficulties. They show up frequently in measles, scarlet fever, etc. Here the tubercular element comes readily to the surface in the form of suppuration of the middle ear. More frequently aroused by fever.

– All blood vessels are abnormal from capillaries to arteries, their walls are all defective and usually unduly dilated.

– Peculiar, carrion-like odour from these aural abscesses is very characteristic.

– Cheesy or curdled discharge.

– If free from ear troubles these children invariably suffer from throat affections, especially tonsils. They appear well in the daytime and free from pain but at night their sufferings begin, and they often scream with earache. They may begin as early as the first year and go on until puberty. The least exposure to cold or slightest draught brings on an attack. Occasionally we have prolonged febrile attacks with great suffering and suddenly better for the an breaking of abscess. Quite often their general health is better even when the ear is discharging copiously of this tubercular, foul smelling pus.

- Ears look pale, white, often cold, and in some cases translucent with the blood vessels enlarged, bluish in colour, or bright red, and their course traceable in the tissues (also in syphilis).
- Eczematous eruptions about the ears, especially the humid eruptions, pustules, fissures and incrustations behind the ear.

NOSE AND SMELL

- Epistaxis profuse, bright red, difficult to arrest and are better by cold applications. Over heating, over exercise will often bring them on.
- The tubercular child will have a haemorrhage from the nose on the slightest provocation – blowing the nose, a slight blow, or even washing the face will produce it in some people.
- Headache, vertigo, congestions to the brain and head ameliorated by nose bleeds.
- In worst forms of hay fever there is much sneezing often depends on the tubercular taint with an acquired latent sycosis engrafted. Discharge soon becomes thick, purulent and sometimes bloody.
- Rush of blood to surface inducing great heat.
- Acne rosacea.
- Catarrhal discharge is thick, usually yellow and of the odour of old cheese or sulphate of hydrogen, and is constantly dropping down the throat.

FACE

- Eyes sunken with blue rings.
- Circumscribed red spot on cheeks, usually appearing afternoon or evening.
- Flushes of heat to face, head and chest.
- Red lips where blood is almost ready to ooze out.
- Reddish millet-sized papules on nose, cheeks, chin and ulcers in corners of mouth.
- Deep fissures in lips.
- In tubercular fever face is pale or with circums-cribed red spots on cheeks. Paleness of face on rising and even after eating. One cheek red, the other pale; one cheek hot, the other cold.
- Tubercular face is round, skin fair, smooth and clear, with waxy smoothness of complexion; eyes bright and sparkling, eyebrows and eye-lashes soft, glossy, long and silken, thin lips.
- There may be high cheek-bones, thick lips and in some cases the skin of the face is rough, voice coarse, deep, often hollow, eyelids red, inflamed, scaly, crusty lashes, broken, stubby, irregularly curved and imperfect. In these cases the syphilitic or tubercular element predominates in latent form.
- The face and head is often seen to be in the shape of a pyramid, with apex at the chin. The nose may be well shaped, the features sharp, eyes usually bright and sparkling, nostrils small, openings narrow and the least obstruction in the nose induces them to breathe through the mouth, which causes an imperfect expansion and filling of the lungs.

- Flushes of heat or circulatory expressions are not evident from the looks of tubercular face; indeed the face looks fairly well even in the last stages of disease, when other parts of the body become emaciated and show marked signs of the disease.

MOUTH

- True ulcers.
- Swelling and induration of glands and such pathological changes as we see taking place in the teeth or dental arches are of a syhilitic or tubercular diathesis.
- Haemorrhage from mouth, excessive bleeding of gums (unless syphilis is actually present) – often they will bleed at slightest touch. Gums recede from teeth or they are soft and spongy. The dental arch is imperfect, irregular, or teeth are imperfect in form, club-shaped, or they come in an imperfect or irregular order, often decaying or becoming carious before they are entirely through the gums. They appear often with much pain and suffering, accompanied with constitutional distur-bances, often of a marked degree, such as diarrhoea, dysentery, spasms, convulsions, febrile states, abscesses of the middle ear, disturbance of digestion, meningeal congestions, and meningeal inflammations. These children cannot endure extremes of heat and cold.

TASTE

- Putrid or taste of blood or pus. Expectoration of pus that taste sweet.
- Salty taste or a rotten-egg taste.

- Taste of blood; it may not come during menstrual period but is present frequently in the morning.
- All metallic tastes make us think of tubercular or syphilitic element.

DESIRES AND AVERSIONS

- Extremists like hot or really cold things.
- Longs for indigestible things – chalk, lime, slate, pencils, etc.
- If the system is not assimilating a certain thing they will crave it (and it is the peculiarity of tubercular patients. – H. Choudhury); this is seen more in young girls, in children and in pregnant women. They are cravers for peculiar things – salt – and will eat it alone from the dish. They eat more salt than all-the family put together. Long for stimulants, beer, wines or hot aromatic things.
- Craves potatoes and meat.
- Desire and cravings for unnatural things to eat, and narcotics such as tea, coffee, tobacco or any other stimulants, have often their origin in psoric or tubercular miasm.

HUNGER

- Faint if hunger is not satisfied or extreme hunger with all-gone, weak, empty feeling in the stomach (but with psoric origin).
- Sometimes constant hunger and eat beyond their capacity to digest, or they have no appetite in the morning but hunger for other meals.

- Great desire for certain things but when he receives them he does not want them; in fact they are repugnant to him (we see this perhaps more in children than in adults).

STOMACH

- Weak, "all-gone" sensation.
- Crave meat, many reject the fat.
- Thrive better on fats and fatty foods; also require much salt. Starches are not easily digested by them.
- Desires salty fish.
- Desires cold things to eat and drink.

CHEST AND LUNGS

- Phthisis - Pulmonary tuberculosis - Consumption.
- The curves and lines of chest are imperfect, the chest is often narrow, lacking width laterally, and depth anteroposteriorly. The subclavicular spaces are hollow or certain areas sunken or pressed, quite often one lung is larger than the other, or the action of one is accelerated and the other lessened; one side is fuller than the other, showing a better development and a greater respiratory area, often lung capacity is reduced and the amount of residual air lessened.
- Breathing is not so full and resonant, although there may be no impediment or obstruction in the air cells of passages. Shoulders are rounded, inclined forward infringing on the chest area, and the free lung action. Poor breathers, they have no desire to take a full respiration, seldom do we find them breathing diaphrag-matically, thus the lung never comes to its fullest expansion and

the air cells are not brought into use and simply become diseased from lack of that life-giving principle they should receive from oxygen. From the lack of work they atrophies and become useless, the least obstruction glues them together and destroy their office.

– Faulty nutrition.

– Afraid of cold air.

– Worse on least exposure to cold.

– Voice coarse, deep with base-like chest tones, throat slightly sore at times, a rawness and a croak – like sound develops in voice; constant desire to hawk or clear throat; of a viscid, scanty mucus (Sore throats of Hep. and Phos.).

– Cough deep – prolonged, worse morning and when patient first lies down in evening. Expectoration purulent, or mucopurulent and in advanced cases, greenish-yellow, often offensive and usually sweetish to taste, or salty (Dependable indications of the combined psoric and syphilitic taints. – R). Sometimes it smells musty or offensive; or it may be bloody or followed by haemorrhage. Cough deep, ringing, hollow, no expectoration or none to speak of.

– Cough can be dry and tight and induce headache or whole body shaken by paroxysms. These people are always full of hope – the last thing that they think of is that they are incurable – or death. Always planning for the future, building castles.

– Glandular changes in cervical region (this often precedes the lung changes). Weakness, anxiety, difficult respiration, laboured respiration.

F - 9

– Sense of great exhaustion, easily tired, never seems to *get* rested; tired at night, tired even after sleep; as the day advances they become better or as the sun ascends their strength revives a little, as it descends they lose it again.

– These patients are often worse in the night – which they dread – and they long for morning. (Look out for patients with the nightly aggravation, no matter what the pathology may be.)

– The tissues are non-resistant, the slightest bruise suppurates – the strong tendency to pus formation. The same may be said of the expectoration of the lungs – its pus-like nature and copiousness.

THE HEART

– A rush of blood to the chest, especially in the young.

– Heart troubles are accompanied with fainting, temporary loss of vision, ringing in the ears, pallor and great weakness worse sitting up and better lying down.

– Cannot climb mountains as disturbed circulation affects brain and they become dizzy and faint, often fainting when they get a rarefied atmosphere. Brain becomes anaemic at a high altitude. Pulse quick, small and thready.

– In these cases, there is gradual failing away of the flesh, rush of blood to the chest and face.

– The dyspnoea is often painful in psoric or tubercular patients.

– The dropsies or the anasarcas of the psoric or tuberculars are always greater than sycotic – they smother or drown the patient before death takes place.

ABDOMEN

- Peritoneal inflammation.
- Often there is worst forms of constipation or inactivity of the bowels in psoric or tubercular patients.
- Beating of the carotids can be felt through abdominal wall.
- Children have ulceration of umbilicus with a yellowish discharge, which smells offensive, carrion-like.
- Menstrual difficulties with reflex pains, spasmodic symptoms and bearing down sensations, especially in tubercular patients. Skin is pale with an underlying bluish tint showing the venous stagnation.
- Hernia – Seldom found outside the tubercular organism. Usually found in flabby, soft-muscles people. Hernia is due to this lack of tone in the muscular system throughout the whole abdominal region. The shape of the tubercular abdomen is saucer-shaped or as a large plate turned bottom side up.

BOWEL AND INTESTINAL TRACT

- Morning aggravation in bowel troubles with sensitivity to cold.
- All gone empty feelings in the abdominal region; sometimes it is a great weakness after stool, felt only in the region of the abdomen (also in psoric cases). General exhaustion or loss of strength a feeling as if all vitality is leaving patient at each evacuation of the bowels.
- True syphilitic or tubercular or cancer patients are worse at night; they are driven out of bed by their diarrhoeas, sometimes this is accompanied with profuse warm or cold perspiration, which is very exhausting and debilitating.

- Tubercular children suffering from bowel troubles tend to develop a sudden brain stasis, or brain metastasis. Sometimes the tubercular manifestations in the brain alternate with a bowel difficulty.
- Verat-a., Ars., Camph. and Cup-m. diarrhoeas and dysenteries are so characteristic in tubercular patients. They look well to-do, have a sudden attack of dysentery and are dead within 48 hours.
- Podo. has painless, copious, yellowish and very offensive stool, worse at night, morning and from milk. *A Tubercular child cannot digest cow's milk in any form.* Least exposure to cold brings on diarrhoea in tubercular children.
- Diarrhoea starts in tubercular babies with first dention associated with defective assimilation of bone-making material.
- Stool of tubercular children may be strongly tainted with sycosis as in Crot-t., Sang., Phos., Kali-c., Tub. and Stann. are quite typical of the tubercular discharges.
- Sometimes in tubercular children stools are ashy or grey in colour showing lack of bile matter. Bloody stools. Child smells musty – mouldy.
- In severe cases of bowel trouble child is fretful, peevish and whiney, does not want to be touched or looked at: marked prostration after stools.
- Aggravation from milk, potatoes, meat and motion.
- Before stool there is often vomiting and retching.
- Stool – with much slimy mucus, or where much blood passes after stool.

- Pin worms or intestinal worms but are found more plentiful in children with tubercular taint.

- Rectal diseases alternating with heart, chest or lung troubles, especially of asthma and respiratory difficulties; e.g., haemorrhoids if operated on or suppressed are followed by lung difficulties or asthma and not infrequently by heart troubles.

- Haemorrhage from rectum.

- Prolapsus of rectum in young children. The bowel difficulties are so frequently accompanied with febrile states, delirium, gastric disturbances, vomiting, purging with exhaustive purging stools.

- In rectum we find many conditions of tubercular origin, as strictures, fistulae, sinuses and pockets (R).

URINARY ORGANS

- Anxiety and much loss of strength after urination.

- In tubercular diathesis, especially in nervous or neurotic patients, urine is pale, colourless and copious.

- Diabetic patients are usually strongly tubercular with diathesis strongly marked.

- Bright's disease.

- Urine offensive and easily decomposed, odour musty, like old hay or foul smelling – even carrion – like.

- In tubercular children urine may be involuntary at night as soon as they fall asleep, also copious. Hence Calc-c. cures as many tubercular miasm tackled.

- Idiopathic hydrocele.

– Loss of the prostatic or seminal fluid leading to prostate trouble and sometimes consumption develops.

– These patients live in gloom with depressed spirits, gloomy forebodings, poor digestion, loss of energy, want of memory. Livid or ashy complexion, appetite often voracious as system calls for more food than it can properly take care of, until the organism fails to perform any function in a proper manner then finally gastric derangements follow.

SEXUAL SPHERE

– Many psyhopathic sexual perversions are especially worse in the tubercular patient.

– Menstruation – exhaustive, often prolonged and copious flow. Haemorrhage bright red, sometimes accompanied with vertigo, faintness, and pallor, worse by rising from recumbent position. Appearing frequently every 2 to 3 weeks; they may or may not be painful but are always exhausting. Feels badly a week before.

– Menses associated with headaches, backaches, gastric disturbances, neuralgias, etc. Occasionally menses appear with diarrhoea, epistaxis, febrile states, optical illusions, roaring in the ears, sensitiveness to noise, loss of appetite, abnormal pains, nausea and bitter vomiting.

– After the flow patient looks pale with dark rings or circles about eyes; or hollow eyes with a warm, exhausted look. Hysterical symptoms often follow menses, of any form or degree in severity and often they are most difficult to treat.

– Flow is often pale, watery and long lasting, as seen in Cal-c, Ferr., etc., or may be bright red.

– Extremities are usually cold and often menstrual flow will induce general anaemia in young women from 17 to 21. They become chlorotic.

– Pale yellowish complexions of ashen hue, accom-panied by starchy or watery leucorrhoeas, palpitation of the heart, faintness and loss of vitality. Later general weakness, flushing in the face, vertigo, ringing in the ears, hoarseness, dry tickling spasmodic cough and finally a true tubercular condition develops. Often they are very sad, gloomy, anxious, full of fanciful notions, forebodings with much fear, extreme sensitiveness, nervous irritability and inclination to weep.

– We sometimes see nausea and vomiting, extreme purging of the bowels, with diarrhoea or dysentery, fainting, cold sweat on the forehead, but flow is seldom clotted; being usually fluid-like, profuse, light red, watery and seldom offensive and it has the odour of fresh blood.

– Leucorrhoea usually purulent but may be watery mucus. Patient often debilitated and worse before flow or immediately after it begins. Deep, thick yellow, or yellowish green. Sometimes lumpy, thick albuminous or purulent. Smelling musty.

– Retroversions, retroflexions and malpositions of uterus. In marked cases of this diathesis uterus is retroverted or retroflexed and many sufferings date from puberty.

– Relaxed muscular system easily exhausted, easily tired, menses copious, too early and long lasting, accompanied with backache, reflexes of all kinds, etc.

– Labours at child birth are often difficult, severe and prolonged and exhausting and many are unable to suckle their children.

UPPER AND LOWER EXTREMITIES

– Neuralgic pains are either psoric or tubercular, often worse motion and better rest, warmth.

– Tubercular miasm effects osseous tissue and nodular growth similar to syphilis. Bones are soft, rickety and curved. Syphilitic element – feet become deformed because legs cannot take weight of body.

– The periosteal difficulties are due to periosteal inflammations or tertiary or tubercular changes in the bones themselves.

– The tubercular and syphilitic bone pains are very similar both to their character and times of aggravation.

– Nails show inflammatory changes due to syphilis and tuberculosis. True onychosis though not of such specific character in the tubercular process as in the tertiary syphilis.

Paronychia is tubercular as met with in pale-skinned, anaemic tubercular subjects. Pustules form often on lower extremities or about fingers or hands.

The nails of these patients are brittle, break or split easily, often hang-nails.

Nails thin as paper, bend easily and are sometimes spoon-shaped – the natural convexity is reversed.

Spotted nails, or white specks – sometimes anterior edges are serrated or slightly scalloped. Often pustular inflammation about the nail. Often nails drop off and grow again.

Periosteal inflammation commonly known as felon or periphalangeal cellulitis.

– Figures are long and do not taper gradually but are blunt of club-shaped at "ends". This long fingered individual with the lengths so irregularly arranged is characteristic. Often hand is thin, soft and flabby and easily compressed, usually very moist or often cold, damp, perspiring profusely.

– The same regarding feet. Coldness of hands and feet is very marked but the patient is not always conscious of it.

– Hang-nails. We see such types in remedies such as *Calc., Bar-c., Bar-i., Iod.* and *Sil.*

– Warm air very annoying, cannot endure much cold neither can they endure much heat.

– Chilblains is a multimiastic disease. There is a tubercular taint, with a sycotic element as a basis – that is why they prove such a dreadful disease producing agent when suppressed by local measures.

– Corns.

– Boils – they may depend on both psoric and tubercular influences.

– Boils with much suppuration.

– Paralytic disease, edematous swellings, anasarca and such are sycotic, syphilitic and tubercular. General muscular weakness and loss of power in ankles.

– Clumsy – awkward, lack of co-ordination – they are always falling. They drop things. They tire easily when walking and especially when climbing a height. Patient is short-winded, climbing stairs tires out the patient.

- White swellings of joints or idiopathic synovitis even rheumatic forms have this tubercular element very marked.

- Drop wrist - weakness or loss of power in tendons about joints. In children and young people, ligaments about joints easily sprained, ankles turn easily from the slightest mis-step, wrist show the same weakness, playing the piano or operating a typewriter causes swelling, soreness or pain in wrist joints. Lack energy as well as strength.

   [Weakness of the ankle joints is a sure indication of the presence of a syphilitic taint in combination of the psoric stigma (R).]

THE SKIN

- Skin affections with glandular involvement will necessarily have the syphilitic or tubercular element.

- In varicose veins the tubercular taint predominates, and it is in these patients that we see the varicose ulcers, the last skin lesion to make its appearance in a case of ancient or hereditary syphilis that has already become, and now is, largely tubercular.

- In ecchymosis or any form of purpura there is a tubercular basis.

- Eczema – Pustule.

- Herpes.

- Urticaria. Bee or bug affect these patients badly.

- Hyperhidrosis and Bromidrosis.

- Abscess and ulcers, esp. following injuries.

- Freckles.

- Fine, smooth, clear skin.

- Goose flesh, (Nat-m., Hep. and Sil. are good examples)
- Impetigo.
- The patients often have benign or malignant tumours.
- In tubercular and syphilitic patients we see much scarring and increase in cicatricial tissue.
- Leprosy.
- In the lymphatic temperament we see the malignan-cies – we find here rich soil for gonorrhoea and syphilis. In tubercular patients we have so much difficulty in eradicating acquired syphilis or gonorrhoea.
- Gonorrhoea runs to gleety discharge and strictures, pockets and metastasis forms, or we have metastasis to ovaries, broad ligaments, tubes, uterus, rectum and all such complications. It is the tubercular diathesis that complicates all skin diseases and makes them so difficult to remove.
- Suppression of any form of ringworm and there often follows tubercular diseases (Burnett).

– Phyllis Speight,
"A Comparison of the Chronic Miasms"

Note :   1.   Pseudo-Psora, means tuberculosis. I have written 'Tuberculosis' instead of the word Pseudo-Psora.

2.	(H)	=	Dr. Hahnemann
	(R)	=	Dr. H. A. Roberts
	(B)	=	Dr. P. N. Banerjee
	(Bnt)	=	Dr. J. C. Burnett
	(P.S.O.)	=	Dr. P. S. Ortega
	(P or P.S.)	=	Dr. Phyllis Speight
	(J.N.K.)	=	Dr. J. N. Kanjilal
	(L)	=	Dr. Lippe.
	(G. V.)	=	Dr. George Vithoulkas

INDICATIONS OF TUBERCULAR
MIASMATIC STATES

(Tubercular and Pre-Tubercular States)

i) Wasting. Loss. Depreciation and destruction.

ii) Cosmopolitan habits. Cosmopolitan – mentally and physically. Mentally keen but physically weak (Lyc.).

iii) Fear of dogs.

iv) Insanity : Acute or chronic with family history of tubercular diseases. True insanity of psora is usually of a tubercular nature.

v) Symptoms are ever-changing. Rapid response to any stimuli, to any slightest change of weather or atmosphere. For that reason it may be called responsive or reacting miasm.

vi) Emaciation inspite of taking proper food and drink.

Eats much but loses flesh rapidly.

The face looks fairly well, even in the last stage of disease, when other parts of the body become emaciated.

vii) Tendency to cough and cold. Catches cold very easily.

viii) History of tuberculosis or any tubercular or lung diseases (like whooping cough, bronchitis, bronchopneumonia, etc.), or ringworm or asthma, asthmatic bronchitis, hay fever or sinusitis.

ix) History of ringworm. Suppression of ringworm.

x) Chronic inflammation of glands and tonsils.

xi) Chronic diarrhoea. Morning diarrhoea with extreme prostration and debility.

xii) Bed-wetting of chronic character. Nocturnal polyuria.

Nocturnal perspiration with or without fever.

xiii) When well – selected medicine fails to relieve or permanently cure.

xiv) "The problem child" – slow in comprehension, dull, unable to keep a line of thought.

Rickets.

Marasmus.

xv) Lean and thin constitution. Fatty constitution with extreme sickness. Fatness without fitness (Calc-c.).

Pigeon chest. Forehead is high.

xvi) Thin hair over scapula. Hair dry, dead, like hemp. Matted hair. Hair grey on the mid-line of the head.

xvii) Nails are thin as paper, with white spot bend easily and sometimes spoon-shaped.

xviii) Epistaxis, bleeding from lungs or rectum with family history of tuberculosis.

HOMOEOPATHIC TREATMENT

As micro – organisms are responsible in psoric, syphilitic and sycotic patients in their primary stage we also find micro-organism or pathogen, namely, Mycobacterium tuberculosis, in tuberculosis patients. Hence we can no longer define tuberculosis as a resultant affect of mixed miasm. Being a separate miasm it has also got its distinct characteristics.

Prolong observations have confirmed in most cases that long continued allopathic treatment can only arrest the tubercular lesion but cannot cure them. Patients suffer from many other complications. Tendency to cough and cold, asthma, diabetes, hyper/hypotension, insanity, bowel troubles, rheumatism and prostration, etc. are after effects in most cases after suppression of tuberculosis.

There is most dependable treatment for tuberculosis in homoeopathy without any side-effects or after effects. It can also alleviate tubercular patients in their tertiary or last stage.

Tuberculosis is not only an acquired but also a hereditary disease. Homoeopathy is the only mode of treatment which can surely save the infants, children and young people from tubercular diathesis like all other chronic dyscrasias.

Miasmatic or constitutional treatment in accordance with the principles of homoeopathy is the only way of treatment for eradicating and preventing tuberculosis.

We cannot think of proper treatment of tuberculosis and all other miasmatic diseases without nosodes. But Acet-ac., Ars., Ferr-m., Hep., Kali-c., Phos., Sil., Stann.,

Sulph., Thyr., Tub., etc., are to be very cautiously prescribed in tuberculosis and even in tubercular patients. These medicines may create undesirable and formidable aggravation.

Being very highly infective disease tuberculosis patients should be isolated from home and public places. Sanatorium is the best resort for them. Proper diet and regimen are inevitable.

In this connection it would not be out of place to mention here that tuberculosis is also a social disease. Although its fundamental cause is tubercular pathogen but its exciting cause is malnutrition – want of proper diet, regimen and sanitation. Mostly it attacks those who have to work more but get little to eat. The people of the unfed and underfed class are the main victim of this destructive disease who are compelled to live beyond the poverty level in the society. *We cannot expect radical cure of tuberculosis and other similar diseases due to malnutrition only by proper treatment. Class society, impregnated with worries, anxiety and tension is one of the great hindrance to cure these sorts of patients. So fight for class less society is not isolated with the fight for eradication of social diseases including tuberculosis. These are inseparable.*

Another important point here is, although demarcation has been drawn between syphilis, tuberculosis and cancer, but all these three diseases are destructive in nature. *Syphilitic dysfunction, tubercular destruction* and *cancerous degeneration have got very meagre difference.* Hence, a child of a syphilitic parent may carry tubercular or cancerous diathesis, a child of tubercular parent may inherit syphilitic or carcinogenic dyscrasia and vice-versa. Transmutation takes place in this way and we are to classify and treat these patients accordingly.

Regarding the exciting and maintaining factors of tuberculosis, cancer and other similar destructive and degenerative diseases, physicians, social & health political workers, teachers and professors should create public awareness through radio, TV, news papers and all other mass-media about the violent reaction and toxic effects of smoking, wine, drug-addiction (like – morphia, heroine, etc., including all intoxicating and narcotic drugs, liquors and other substances), ill-effects of rich food, cold and soft drinks, cosmetics, contraceptives, etc. They should also educate people about pollutions and debauchery. The exploiters of feudo-capitalist society very cunningly conspire and entice our younger generation to demoralize them by throwing into such pseudo-cultural life, mainly to divert their struggling zeal and revolutionary spirit. So everybody should be cautious about the said exciting causes of those dreadful diseases if he does not want to be their victim. The following chapter gives us useful hints in treating tubercular patients.

SOME IMPORTANT HINTS
FOR TREATMENT OF TUBERCULOSIS
(Phthisis Pulmonalis)

ACUTE STATE (Phthisis Florida)

(A) Ferr-p., Ham., Mill., Puls., Senec., Sil., Ther.

(B) Ars., Bry., Chin., Cimic., Dulc., Hep., Kreos., Med., Phos., Sang., Sulph.

ACUTE EXACERBATIONS IN ALL STAGES

(B) Kali-n.

ACUTE TUBERCULOSIS FROM SUPPRESSED MENSES

(A) Senec.

COLD DAMP WEATHER

(B) Dulc.

COUGH

(B) Ars-i., Bell., Cod., Cor-r., Dros., Hep., Hyos., Kali-c., Nit-ac., Phos., Sil., Stann.

DEBILITY

(B) Ars-i., Chinin-ar., Psor., Zinc-m.

DIARRHOEA

(B) Arn., Ars-i., Ars., Chin., Crot., Cupr-ar., Phos-ac., Phos., Bapt.

DIGESTIVE DISORDERS AND LIVER DISTURBANCE

(B) Cupr-ar., Hydr., Nux-v.

(C) Chel.

DYSPNOEA

(C) Carb-v., Ip., Phos.

F - 10

EMANCIATION

(B) Abrot., Arg-n., Ars-i., Calc., Dros., Hydr., Iod., Lyc., Nat-m., Ol-j., Phos-ac., Sanic., Syph., Thuj., Tub., Verat.

FEVER

(B) Bapt., Chinin-ar., Ferr-p.

(C) Ars-i., Calc-i., Chin., Chinin-s., Iod., Lyc., Nit-ac., Phos., Sang., Sil., Stann.

HEMOPTYSIS

(HAEMORRHAGES)

(B) Acal., Achil., Acon., Chin., Ferr-ac., Ferr-p., Ham., Ip., Mill., Phos., Trill.

INCIPIENT

(A) Ars-i., Calc., Calc-p., Dros., Hep., Kali-c., Kali-p., Lyc., Med., Ol-j., Phos., Psor., Puls., Senec., Sil., Stann., Tub.

(B) Acet-ac., Agar., Bry., Carb-v., Dulc., Ferr., Lach., Nat-s., Rumx., Sang., Sulph., Ther.

INCIPIENT TUBERCULOSIS AFTER INJURY TO THE CHEST

(A) Ph-ac.

(B) Ruta.

(C) Mill.

INSOMNIA

(B) Coff.

(C) All-s., Dig., Sil.

LAST STAGE

(A) Calc.,Carb-v., Lach., Lyc., Puls., Sang., Tarent.

LYING ON SIDE AGGRAVATES

(C) Calc.

MENTAL SHOCK, FROM
Arn., Ign., Nat-m., Ph-ac.

MINERS' TUBERCULOSIS FROM COAL DUST
(C) Carb-s.

NIGHT SWEATS IN TUBERCULAR PATIENT
(B) Acet-ac., Agar., Ars., Chin., Jab., Ph-ac., Phos., Sil.

NURSING MOTHERS
(B) Kali-c.

OLD PEOPLE
(B) Nat-s.

PAINS IN CHEST
(B) Bry., Kali-c.,

(C) Acon., Calc.,Cimi., Guaj., Myris., Phos., Pix.

PITUITOUS
(A) Ant-c., Ant-t., Con., Ferr-p., Hep., Kali-i., Kali-chl., Lyc., Med., Phos., Psor., Sang., Senec., Stann., Ther.

(B) Aesc., Bar-m., Coc-c., Dulc., Ferr., Kali-c., Kreos., Lach., Merc. Merc-c., Nat-s., Puls., Seneg., Sil., Sulph.

PURULENT AND ULCERATIVE
(A) Calc., Iod., Kali-c., Lyco., Phos.

(B) Ars., Ars-i., Carb-an., Carbn-s., Carb-v., Dros., Hep., Kali-m., Kali-p., Lach., Merc., Nit-ac., Plb., Psor., Puls., Sil., Sulph.

SYCOTIC
(A) Aur., Calc., Lyc., Med., Nat-s., Nit-ac., Thuj.

(B) Aur-m., Carb-an., Caust., Dulc., Lach., Phyt., Puls., Sil., Ther.

SORE MOUTH

(C) Lach.

STONE-CUTTERS TUBERCULOSIS

(B) Calc., Sil.

(C) Lyc., Puls.

Note :

1. There are also more remedies in grade 'C' which have not been quoted in many places being less important.

2. (A) – 'A'/1st Grade.

   (B) – 'B'/2nd Grade.

   (C) – 'C'/3rd Grade.

"In the long run Hahnemann's miasmatic conception turn out to be that of infection as it is understood in orthodox medicine. From this point of view his psora theory, forms in point of fact, not only a completion of the law of similars, but also an improvement and a perfection of the homoeopathic science of healing in general, and indeed the coping stone in Hahnemann's structure of healing art."

– B.K. Sarkar, Ibid, P. 362

ANTI-TUBERCULAR REMEDIES

'A' Grade : Agar., Ars-i., Aur., Bac., Calc., Calc-p., Carc., Euon., Hep., Hydr., Iod., Kali-c., Kali-chl., Kali-i., Kali-p., Kali-s., Lyco., Medo., Nat-s., Phos., Psor., Puls., Scir., Senec., Sep., Sil., Spong., Stann., Sulph., Syph., Tarent., Ther., Thuj., Tub., Zinc.

'B' Grade : All-c., Ant-c., Ant-i., Ant-t., Acet-ac., Ars., Aviare., Bapt., Bar-m. Brom., Bry., Bufo. Calc-i., Calc-s., Carb-an., Carb-s., Carb-v. Cetr., Chinin-ar., Chin., Con., Crot-t., Dros. Dulc., Elaps., Ferr-ar., Ferr-i., Ferr-p., Fl-ac., Gal-ac., Graph., Guaj., Kali-n., Kreos., Lac-d., Lach., Lachn., Laur., Merc., Myos., Nux-v., Nat-c., Nat-m., Nat-sel., Nit-ac., O1-j., Phel., Ph-ac., Plb., Polyg-a., Sang., Seneg., Sep.

REFERENCE

K - Rep.	:	P. 878-9
L- Rep.	:	P. 266
PH - Rep.	:	P. 64
Boericke - Rep.	:	P. 900
	and	

Personal experience of the author.

8. CHRONIC MIASM – CANCER

INTRODUCTION

Cancer is considered under the domain of neoplastic disease. It is a malignant tumour devoid of surrounding fibrous capsule and may invade and destroy the tissue in which it arises. It possesses an unlimited power of disorderly reproduction of cells or tissues of variable codes of proliferation. Malignant tumours are capable of producing metastasis or secondary growth at a distant site from the primary location. These are classified according to the site of primary growth into two broad categories – carcinomas and sarcomas.

Carcinoma is a malignant growth derived from epithelial cells (or cells similar to the skin or the mucus membrane lining the stomach, bowel or glands) and it tends to infiltrate the surrounding tissues and to give rise to metastasis.

Sarcoma is a malignant tumour developing in the connective tissues of the bone, muscle and tendon. In other words, sarcoma – a tumour made up of a substance like the embryonic connective tissue, tissue composed of closely packed cells embedded in a fibrillar or homogeneous substance.

THE AETIOLOGY AND
CLASSIFICATION OF CANCER

It is not known till to-day how exactly the tumours are produced and what are the agents that are capable of producing them. Factors which are believed to be responsible for the development of malignant growth in men and animals could be either chemical, physical or hormonal in nature. Some scientists believe that Polyoma virus, Semian virus and human Adeno virus are responsible for cancer (A.B. Patrika, 4.7.1986). Moreover, EB virus, HS virus and C-Type RNA virus, etc., have been associated with different types of cancer.

Cancer may be classified in number of ways as follows:

1. Aetiological Classification

Cancer due to occupational hazards; ecological and environmental factors ; excessive smoking; genetic factors and virual (as in Burkitt's Lymphoma).

2. Regional Classification

Cancer of muscles, bones, skin and internal organs.

3. Histological Classification

(a) *Actual Teratoma* (Extra body tumour, e.g., testis and ovary).

(b) *Blastoma* : Hyaloma related to connective tissues and *Lepidoma* – related to epithelial tissue.

Hyaloma epiblast (C.N.S.) is Spongioblastoma.

Primary – e.g.,   Round Cell,
                    Spindle Cell,
                    Mixed Cell.

Secondary – e.g., Fibrosarcoma,
Chondrosarcoma,
Liposarcoma,
Myosarcoma.

Lepidoma epiblast (carcinoma)

(i) Basal cell carcinoma

(ii) Squamous cell carcinoma

(iii) Adeno carcinoma

(iv) Scirrhous cell carcinoma and Encephaloid Cell carcinoma.

(v) Malignant melanoma.

Lepidoma mesoblasts

(i) Haemangioendothelioma

(ii) Lymphangioendothelioma.

(c) *Teratoblastoma*

It is a combination of both teratoma and blastoma.

VARIETIES OF SARCOMA

(1) **Histological Classification**

(a) Fibrosarcoma : Here fibroblast tends to differentiate into fibrous connective tissue. Clinically it is graded as I, II & Ill of which grade II is more malignant and grade III is of little practical value.

(b) Chondrosarcoma : It develops from cartilage, remnants of bone.

(c) Osteosarcoma.

(d) Liposarcoma.

(e) Fibromyosarcoma.

(f) Neurosarcoma.

(2) **Cytological Classification**

    (a) Spindle cell sarcoma, e.g., Fibrosarcoma.

    (b) Round cell sarcoma.

    (c) Mixed cell sarcoma.

    (d) Giants cell sarcoma.

(3) **Sarcoma of Haemopoietic tissues**

    (a) Lymphosarcoma.

    (b) Reticulum cell sarcoma.

MECHANISM OF SPREAD

Spreading of malignant cell is mainly due to high rate of multiplication, amoeboid activity with the help of its pseudopodia, enzymatic activity of fibrinolysin, hyaluronidase and collagenase, thromboplastic activity and phagocytic activity.

Routes

    (i) Direct infiltration of the malignant cells to the intracellular spaces and intermuscular spaces. Direct local spread by lymphatics as emboli - e.g. carcinoma of breast, gall bladder, etc., prefer this route.

    (ii) Spread by metastasis

        (a) Malignant cells enter into the vessel and follow path of vessel causing fibrosis in the vessel. This permeation causes pain and severe pain takes place when the nerve endings around the vessels are compressed by fibrous tissue. This permeation is known as lymphatic permeation.

(b) Carcinomatus cells in late stage spread through blood channel and embolus lodge in lung, liver and any vital organ of the body. Veins involvements here as venous embolism and venous permeation are common.

iii) Transplantation of cells from one individual to another.

(iv) Implantation of cells :

(a) Apposition from lip to lip, cervix to vagina, bladder to adjacent area, etc.

(b) Transcoelomic implantation, e.g., – stomach to peritoneal sac.

(c) Direct implantation: Needle which is used for the liver biopsy causes metastasis during aspiration.

FACTORS RESPONSIBLE FOR CANCER

1. Incidence of carcinoma increases with the increase of age (after 40 years), sarcoma is common in early age (in young age).

2. Certain chemicals like asbestos, vinyl chloride and benzphyrene.

3. Occupational exposure to carcinogens, such as X-ray, radioactive substances.

4. Certain virus (as in Burkitt's Lymphoma).

5. Factors related to diet, smoking and genetic factors.

EARLY SIGNS OF CANCER

(i)   Prolong unusual bleeding or discharge from any orifice of body.

(ii)   A wound/lesion that does not heal.

(iii) A change in bladder or bowel habits.

(iv)   A lump or thickening in the breast or elsewhere.

(v)   Discolouration of skin (Black).

(vi)   Persistent hoarseness, cough or spitting of blood.

(vii) Persistent indigestion or dysphagia.

(viii) A change in a wart or mole.

So-called modern medicine suggests administration of hormone therapy in selected cases, e.g., administration of oestrogens in prostatic carcinoma; destruction of tumour cells selectively without producing irreversible changes in other tissues and surgical removal in many cases specially in early stage. Irradiation with suitable X-ray or radiation from radio active substances is suggested in many cases. Chemotherapy is also suggested. Ultimate is careful control to avoid undue effects on other rapidly dividing cells such as the bonemarrow.

Heredity : While there is very little predisposition to most of the common types of tumours, there are a number of uncommon neoplastic diseases which are inherited.

Why cancer is more difficult to cure

According to Wilson and Gisvold's text book of organic medicinal and pharmaceutical chemistry, edited by Robert F. Doerge, Ph. D. there are cognate reasons why cancer is more difficult to cure than bacterial infections. One is that there are qualitative differences between human and bacterial cells. For examples, bacterial cells have distinctive cell walls and their ribosomes are different from those of human cells. In contrast, the differences between normal and neoplastic human cells are merely quantitative. Another difference is that immune mechanisms and other host defences are very important in killing bacteria and other foreign cells, whereas they play a negligible role in killing cancer cells. By their very nature, the cancer cells have eluded or overcome the immune surveillance system of the body. Suppose that a patient had a trillion leukemia cells. This amount would cause a serious debilitation. A potent anticancer drug might reduce this population 10,000 fold, in which case the symptoms would be alleviated and the patient would be in a state of remission. However, the remaining hundred million leukemia cells could readily increase to the original number of therapy. Furthermore, a higher proportion of resistant cells would be present, which would mean that retreatment with the same agent would achieve a lesser response than before.

DIAGNOSIS OF CANCER

To determine malignancy three criteria are to be kept in mind :

(i) Margin : On histological study, cell invasion to the adjacent tissue must be present.

(ii) Structure : Now – resemblance of structure of the malignant tumour to the parent tissue.

(iii) Cell: It has some special features such as,

    (a) Change in shape and size of cells.

    (b) Anisonucleosis, e.g., change in shape, size and mitotic condition of the nuclei.

    (c) Loss of polarity.

    (d) Anaplasis: Cells fail to produce the structure of parent tissue.

Clinical methods to diagnose are physical examination, endoscopy, radiography and biopsy. Biopsy is for confirmation. To obtain better result in treatment early detection is desired. But still the vigilant eye of the clinician is the best diagnostic apparatus.

Endoscopy : In helps to note any anatomical change, locate lesion and to locate the spot for such biopsy.

Radiography : Barium meal examination, arteriography, lymphangiography and tomography are done with X-ray.

Biopsy :   (i) Needle biopsy – As the cells are loosely packed, it is drawn by aspiration and specially stained.

        (ii) Scrape biopsy – This is done from raw surface for exfoliative cytology to demonstrate malignant cells.

        (iii) Punch biopsy.

        (iv) Cutting biopsy – these two are helpful to know the type of tumour.

Oncologists are now taking help of tomography, mammography, radioactive isotope scanning and genetic – engineering techniques to diagnose early and to treat the cases.

A decade ago, scientists showed that a class of enzymes could be used to cut, move, recombine and decipher DNA (deoxyribonucleic acid). With these "gene-splicing" or recombinant DNA techniques, scientists can now locate cancer at its source. And they have proved that cancer is the result of an error in our genetic programme. The gene error appears to be inherited in some cases. Carcinogens and on very rare occasions, virus attack our DNA. As a result, the normal genes in our bodies can quickly be changed into cancer-causing agents or oncogenies.

"Once the oncogene gets going", says Dr. Weinberge, "it wreaks havoc in the cell... and the end result is cancer". Scientists suspect that relatively few genes may be responsible for many cancers. Using recombinant DNA technology, they have tracked down about half a dozen human oncogenies, at least one has been implicated in cancers of both lung and large intestline.

In 1975, scientists at Medical Research Council in Cambridge, England, succeeded in fusing a myeloma cell with an antibody producing white blood corpuscle. The resulting hybridoma (a contraction of hybrid-myeloma) inherited the ability to manufacture one specific antibody from the white-cell parent and the ability to proliferate indefinitely outside the body from the cancer side of the family. It will go on dividing for ever, making exact clones of itself that will produce one extraordinarily pure type of antibody, known as monoclonal. When many cancers reach the advanced stage, nothing works better than surgery or radiation to reduce the sheets bulk of the tumour mass. The problem is the few stray cancer cells that escape such measures ... for even this small foot-hold is sufficient to launch a new offensive as the cancer cells divide and multiply.

Both before and after treatment, the question of metastasis ... the spreading of cancer cells to distant locations within the body ... remains crucial. Monoclonal antibodies may be able to serve additionally as powerful diagnostic tools that allow the exact size and location of these treacherous growth to be mapped.

INDICATIONS OF CANCER AND
PRE-CANCEROUS STATES

i)   Any ulceration in the mouth or in any mucous membrane which has a chronic tendency, which does not heal. Any ulceration of non-healing type anywhere in the organism.

Any degenerative disease.

Unexplained and persistent or increasing pain in the body or limbs.

ii) Any tumour in the chest. Any palpable mass or lump in the breast.

iii) Any tumour/growth/malformation/excrescence/ gland in any part of the body starts with pain. Any painless lump or thickening in the breast, lip or tongue.

iv) Chronic dysphagia i.e. difficulty in swallowing.

v)   Chronic Hoarseness. Unexplained cough. Nagging cough.

vi) Haemorrhage from any part of the body without any reason. Regular bleeding from the nipple or any other body orifice. Painless, intermittent, easy discharge of blood. Unusual bleeding or discharge.

vii) Haemorrhage at the time of intercourse.

viii) Chronic dyspepsia and loss of appetite. Any change in the normal bowel habit, e.g., urging for stool at odd hours. Sudden change in urination, e.g., micturition/inability to retain urine even for short time. In short, change in bowel and bladder habit.

ix) Crops of warts/condylomata/moles/birth marks or sudden and progressive change in their colour or size.

F-11

Progressive anaemia or emaciation without any apparent cause.

x) Black or blackish discoloration of skin or tongue.

xi) Excessive fear and apprehensions. Melancholia. Fear of death. Fear of disease. Extreme despair of recovery. Aggravation at night, rest and when alone. Company ameliorates. Extreme prostration. Contradictory states of mind and body. Contradictory modalities, desires and aversions. Amelioration by slow movement and activities.

xii) Chronic insomnia without any apparent cause.

Unremitting or long-continued fever not responding to any treatment. Glandular fever.

xiii) Family history of sarcoma or carcinoma. Family history of cancer, diabetes, tuberculosis, pernicious anaemia or a combination of these (Carcinosinum).

xiv) History of more than three infective diseases. Personal history of whooping cough or other severe acute infection at an early age.

xv) When well-selected medicine does not give any relief or expected result.

xvi) Cancerous affections, malignant growths and such diseases have all the miasms present, especially the sycotic and the tubercular combined. Psora can never be left out of malignancies, no matter what other element may combine with, it fathers them all (P.S.).

TREATMENT

Though the exact aetiology of cancer is yet to be explored but its distinct characteristic compels us to accept it as a separate miasm which I have stated elsewhere. Some of us are of the opinion that so long its causative factor has not been found out, it may be considered as the resultant effect of mixed-miasm.

In this connection we are also to judge whether *repeated suppression of other miasmatic diseases with massive doses of so-called modern drugs are responsible for resulting in a revolt of the organism in the form of this most complicated, deadly state of disease like cancer.* It may also be considered till to-day as the ultimate state of all chronic diseases. People become panic-stricken on hearing the very name of CANCER as they think that it has got no answer.

In homoeopathy there is enormous scope for its treatment. In most cases of its primary stage, also maximum cases of secondary stage there is sure, safe and salutary curative treatment by homoeopathy. Even in tertiary stage of carcinoma or sarcoma there is dependable alleviative treatment by homoeopathy. We can control tremendous pain, burning and discharges of this dreadful disease by homoeopathic medicine. Eminent classical homoeopaths of the world are rendering yeoman's service in curing and controlling of cancer from the very inception of homoeopathy.

In this connection it will not be out of place to mention here that hereditary and genetic cancerous diathesis of infants, children and younger ones can only be eradicated and transformed into healthy state ONLY by homoeopathic treatment which has opened a new vista in the history of medicine. So homoeopathy has a very sure, certain and reliable answer against the scourge of this terrible and fearful disease of mankind. Prevention of cancer is possible only by suitable, continued homoeopathic treatment. We are to deal with these cases as we do in all other chronic diseases. In many patients I have been getting expected results, even sometime magical results, in alleviating and in leading the cancer patients towards the road to recovery by strictly following the Hahnemannian principles. In this connection it is also to be borne in mind that palliative or suppressive treatment by poly prescription or mixed medicines in any case, as done to-day by more than 95% of homoeopaths due to lack of proper learning, is a crime.

Another tragedy is that some of them are also claiming good results and thus creating illusion in our homoeopathic society. My humble question, "If your claim is at all correct then what is the difference between classical homoeopathy and psedo-homoeopathy? Have all the laws and doctrines of homoeopathy become obsolete? "Please beware of pseudo-homoeopaths."

We all are aware of the fact that there is also limitation in homoeopathy. We cannot expect satisfactory results in those cases where there will be (1) want of dependable characteristic symptoms, or (2) adverse reaction to the well selected remedy, or lack of vitality of the patient. Most of these cases are incurable. In this connection we should not forget about *the spontaneous cure of cancer,* although number of such cures are limited.

Dr. Kanjilal's Opinion

The following suggestions regarding treatment of cancer patients by our reverend Dr. J.N. Kanjilal are invaluable which will guide us in dealing with cancer cases. He says :

"The difficulty in finding the curative similium is due to failure in tracing out the significant points (Aphorism 5, Organon) or dependable characteristics revealing the fundamental miasmatic stigmata; and even if any such is ferreted out, difficulty in administering the similimum, in view of the probability, of formidable, occasionally may lead to fatal aggravation."

"A case may reach to such a stage of (a) Paucity of dependable characteristic individualizing symptoms, or (b) Adverse reaction to the similimum owing to the following factors :

(i) The disease having advanced too far to its ultimates.

(ii) Various endogenous and exogenous maintaining causes :

(a) Endogenous causes – Various contradictions, disappointments, worries, anxieties, shocks, etc., of modern life as well as low vitality due to perversed and preternatural life of modern civilization.

b) Exogenous causes – Denatural foods, drinks and atmosphere particularly vitiated by excessive cosmic fall-outs caused by repeated atomic explosions.

(iii) Iatrogenic – The lavish use of various highly potent suppressive modern drugs of the orthodox school for all and sundry indispositions (like anxiety, insomnia, constipation, headache, etc.), or diseases, acute as well as chronic. The older endemics of malaria, etc., as well as the various older epidemic diseases seem now-a-days to have been replaced by more malicious conditions like hypertension, coronary disease, tuberculosis, cancer, etc., in endemic form. The average life-span has, of course, much increased, but that at serious cost of general vitality.

"Despite all these factors, it is invariably found that if the case comes to the care of a true Hahnemannian, homoeopath in proper time, that is, in a stage when at least some of the individualizing characteristic symptoms of the case are still persisting, when the case is just tending towards cancerous (not yet definitely diagnosable) or above the initial stage of diagnosed cancer, the adverse tendency can definitely be reversed towards the path of cure."

"But the term 'Cure' should be used with some reservation, if we want to use it in a truly homoeopathic sense. The highest ideal of cure, as given in the aphorism 2 of the Organon, in this disease condition (or for the matter of that, various other formidable disease conditions of the percentage), can be achieved only by joint and organized efforts of a large section of the physicians. Strictly following the principles of homoeopathy and seriously endeavouring to eradicate and annihilate the fundamental (miasmatic) cause (hereditary as well as acquired) and environmental causes for some generations."

"The best that we, homoeopaths of the world, can do for this and similar diseases in the todays prevailing situation, is to take the following steps with all seriousness :

(1) We must treat all the cases of any disease coming to our care, with meticulous attention

to the fundamental (miasmatic) cause, hereditary as well as acquired. This applies particularly
to the cases of infants and children, having a
tendency to develop such ultimates in future life.
We should train ourselves enough to foresee and
diagnose these tendencies even in infancy and
childhood.

(2) We must scrupulously eschew the methods of
palliation and suppression, as done today, by
more than 90% of homoeopaths themselves by
using various forms of palliatives on merely
partial indications.

(3) We must not get nervous or frightened to accept
cases of diagnosed cancer (or similar diseases),
as in most of these cases it is only true
homoeopathy, which can do better than any
other system of medicine, at least to relieve the
troubles of the case and to prolong the life with
greater care, and to save the poor victim from
the drastic suppressive measures with various
consequent trouble – some side effects, at great
financial cost.

(4) All the homoeopaths of the world must unite and
make a systematic and organized efforts to
convince the public, the executive authorities, as
well as the practitioners of the orthodox school
about the really effective, radical and above all
rational (homoeopathic) approach to cancer,
about the dangers of denaturalization of food,
etc., and pollution of all environmental conditions
as is being rampantly done in the present phase
of civilization, also about the futility or rather
menaceful irrationality of the waste of so much

money and labour for discovering more and more potent measures for suppressing the ultimates of cancerous condition as well as various other fatal diseases of the present age".*

Thus homoeopathy renders most vital and positive role in cancer. Of course we should leave no stone unturned for further research and progress of homoeopathy so that we can be more successful in treating and preventing cancer and similar destructive diseases.

* Kanjilal Dr. J.N. : Writings on Homoeopathy: pp. 206- 210.

DIET AND REGIMEN

Uncooked or half-cooked substances and fruits have been suggested for cancer patients by many authorities. Many scientists say that vegetables, especially green vegetables are more helpful. Little fish or chicken may be allowed. Fats and fatty things, salt and sugar should · be controlled as far as possible. Half-boiled or water-poach eggs may be given. Rich food and drinks, cold drinks, overeating should not be allowed. Smoking of all sorts, all intoxicating drugs, liquors, or substances (like-morphia, opium, heroin etc., tobacco of all kinds), all sorts of debaucheries, irregularities should be strictly prohibited. Anxiety and tension are always harmful for these patients. Tolerable exercise or morning walk, light amusement, rest and recreation are extremely necessary for all patients. The following regimen may be helpful to the ailing mankind, especially to all patients of destructive nature like cancer, tuberculosis, diabetes, hypertension etc. :

(1) Suitable/tolerable exercise, morning walk, particularly on a grassy field.

(2) Take bath in normal/natural cold water or luke-warm water daily.

(3) Should give-up the habit of smoking, tobacco chewing, drugging, drinking of alcohol, coffee or other intoxicating substances. From various experimentations it has been clearly known that all smokers run the risk of lung cancer that is ten times higher than in non-smokers. It is also to be noted that chewing of tobacco in any form is one of the exciting cause of oral cancer.

(4) Avoid as far as possible all irritating and exciting matters. Worry, anxiety and tension should also be avoided. Should not lose temper even under provocation. Avoid hurry and sudden exertion.

(5) Proper rest and recreation.

(6) Strong self-confidence that I will be cured.

(7) Patient should not be informed about the severity of his disease.

(8) Excessive use of salt, sugar and fat, rich, spicy and warm food, condiments, cold drink over feeding, chemical cosmetics should be avoided. Meat, especially fatty flesh should also be avoided.

(9) Food should be taken at regular hours. Easily digestible, good whole-some food like – Oats, Brown bread, Maize, Apples, Nuts, Almond, Milk, Honey, Grapes, Black Molasses, Green and leafy vegetables, Food rich in potash content, uncooked or half cooked substances, small fishes, etc., are very suitable.

(10) To observe fasting at least once a week.

(11) To take rest for 30 minutes after lunch.

(12) To go to bed at regular hours.

(13) To avoid suppression of external manifestation like eruption, eczema, etc., by external application.

(14) For mental tranquility, readings of progressive books, periodicals, news paper may be allowed. Tolerable healthy activities on matters of national and international affairs for peace and

progress of mankind are very helpful. Pseudo-cultural, vested interested activities are always detrimental to human health.

In this respect it is important to mention that our struggle against cancer and all other similar dreadful diseases can not be successful only with well selected medicine or treatment. Proper diet, regimen and suitable environment, etc., are extremely necessary. The movement for health would be crowned with success when there would be no obstacle to recovery. Hence, *our struggle for health is not at all isolated from our movement for a world free from wars, weapons and exploitations.*

IMPORTANT HINTS FOR
TREATMENT OF CANCER

The following hints may be helpful in finding out the similimum :

Cancer of antrum — Aur., Symph.

Cancer of axilla — Ars-i., *Aster.,* Carb-an.

Cancer of bone — Fl-ac., Aur., Aur-i., Con., Calc-f., Calc., Calc-hp., Hep., Hecl., Lyc. Nit-ac., *Phos.,* Sil., Symph., Syph., Thuj., Ther.

Cancer of bone, femur — Stront.

Cancer of bowel — Lob-e.

Cancer of bowel, lower — Lyc., Ruta, Tarax.

Cancer of breast (Mammae) — Alum., *Apis,* ARG-N., Arn., ARS., Ars-i., *Aster., Aur.,* Aur-m-n. *Bad.,* Bar-i., Bell., Bell-p., *Brom.,* Bry., BUFO., Cadm-i., Cadm-s., Calc., *Carb-ac., Carb-an.,* Carb-s., Carb-v., *Carc.,* Caust., Cham., *Chin.,* Cist., *Clem.,* Coloc., CON. COND., Dios., Ferr-i., Form-ac., *Gali.,* GRAPH, Hep., *Hydr.,* Iod., Kali-c., Kali-i., Kreos., Lac-c., *Lach.,* Lyc.,MERC., Merc-i-f., Nat-cac., Nit-ac., Ol-an., *Ox-ac., Phos. Phyt.,* Plb-i., *Psor.,* Puls, *Sang., Scir.,*

		Scroph., Sep., SIL., *Sulph.,* *Thuj,* Thiosin., Tub.
Cancer of Caecum	–	Orni.
Cancer of Cervix	–	Cadm-s., Con., Dios., Hydr.
Cancer of Clavicles, fungus acmatodes	–	*Ars.,* Calc-c., Carb-an., *Kreos., Lach., Lyc., Merc., Nit-ac.,* Phos., Sep., *Sil., Sulph., Thuj.*
Cancer of Eye	–	Aur-mu., CALC., LYC. PHOS., Sep., Sil., Thuj.
Epithelioma (or Cancer of epithelial tissues, i.e., Carcinoma)	–	Cond., Lach.
of Cornea	–	Hep.
of Lids	–	Hydr., Lach., Phyt., Thuj.
of Lower Lids	–	Apis, Cund, Thuj.
of Lachrymal Gland	–	Carb-an.
Cancer of Face	–	ARS., *Aur., Carb-an., Con., Kali-ar.,* Phos.
Cancer of Genitalia	–	Ars., Bell., Carb-an., CON., Phos., Phyt., Sil., Spong., Thuj.
Cancer of Bladder	–	Apis, Arg-m., Ars., Ars-m., Cund.,Ham.,Tarax., Thlas., Thuj.
Cancer of Penis	–	Ars., Bell., Canth., *Carb-an.,* Carb-s., Chrom., Con., Lach., Phos., Phyt., Sil., Spong., *Thuj.*
of Scrotum (epithelioma)	–	Carb-an., Phos-ac.
of Scirrhus	–	Carb-an.

of Testes	– Arn., Carb-an., Clem., Fuli., Lach., Ox-ac., Thuj., Sil., Spong.
Cancer of Glandular Structure	– ARS., *Aur-m.*, BUFO,. *Carban.*, Cist-c., *Con.*, Hochst., Iod., Nit-ac., SULPH.
Cancer of Intestine	– Apis, Ars., Bell., Carb-ac., Carb-v., Grap., Hep., Hydn., Kreos., Lach., Lob., Nit-ac., Orni., Phos., Sep., Sil., Sulph., Thuj.
Cancer of Larynx	– Ars., Lach., Merc., Nit-ac., Phos., Sang., Thuj.
Cancer of Lips	– *Ars., Aur-m., Carb-an., Cic., Cist.,* CON., *Kreos., Lach., Lyc., Sep.,* Sil.
Cancer of Lower Lips	– Acet-ac., Ars., Ars-i., Calc., Cund., *Cist., Clem., Con.,* Graph., Hydr., Kreos., Lyc., Phos., Phyto., Sep., Sil., Thuj.
Cancer of Lips due to pressure of pipe	– Con., Sep.
Cancer of Lips due to smoking	– Con.
Cancer of Lungs	– Ars., *Ars-i.,* Brom., *Carb-an.,* Carb-v., Cob., Crot., Hipp., Kali-c., Kali-i., *Kreos.,* Phos., Sang., Sec., Ther.
Cancer of Gums	– Carb-v., Cist., Hecla, Hydr., Kreos., Merc., Merc-c., Nit-ac., Sil., Lach.,

Cancer of Mouth	– Kreos., Merc-c., Nit-ac.
Cancer of Mucus Membrane	– Ant-m., Lob-e.
Cancer of Nose	– *Ars.,* AUR., Aur-m., Calc., Carb-ac., Carb-an., Chr- ac., Kreos., Lac-c., Merc., Hydr., Kali-s., Kali-bi., Phyt., Sep., Sil., Sulph.
Cancer of Omentum	– Lob.
Cancer of Ovaries	– Apis, Ars., Calc., Carb-an., Con:, Graph., Kreos., Lac-c., Lach., Psor., Sil., Thuj.,
Cancer of Palate	– Aur., Cinnab., Crot-h., Hydr., Kali-bi., Merc-c., Merc-cy., Nit-ac., Tarax.
Cancer of Prostate Gland	– Crot., Carc., Hydrang., Kali-cy., Sabal.
Cancer of Pylorus	– Iris.
Cancer of Rectum	– Alum., Ars., Iod., Laur., Nit-ac., Phyt., Ruta., Sang., Sep.
Cancer of Sternum	– Ars-s-r., Sulph.
Cancer of Stomach (also of Liver and Gall Bladder, or Carcinoma Hepatitis)	– Acet-ac., Alum., Arg-n., ARS, *Bell.,* BISM., Cadm-s., Cad-m., Calc., Caps., CARB-AC., Carb-v., Card-m., Cham., Chelin., CHOL., CON., Cund., Crot-h., Germ-m., HYDR., *Iris.,* Kali-b., *Kreos.,* Lach., Lyc., *Merc-c. Mez.,* Nux-v., Orni., Plb., Plb-i., PHOS., Sec., *Sep.,* Sil., Staph., Sulph., Ther.

Cancer of Throat	– Carb-an., Lach., Led., Tarent.
Cancer of Tongue	– Alumn., *Apis*, ARS., *Aur.*, *Aur-m.*, Benz-ac., Calc., Carb-ac., *Carb-an.*, Caust., Cit-ac., *Con.*, Chr-ac., Crot-h., Cund., Fuli., *Gali.,Hydr.*, Kali-bi., Kali-chl., Kali-cy., *Kali-i.*, Lach., *Mur-ac.*, Nit-ac., Nux-v., *Phos.*, *Phyt.*, Rad-br., Semp-v., Sep., *Sil.*, Sulph., Thuj.
Cancer (Malignant Tumour) of Uterus	– Alum., Alumn., Anac., Apis, *Arg-m.,Arg-n.*, ARS., ARS-I., Aur., Aur-m-n., Brom., *Bufo*, Cadm-s., Calc-ar., Calc., Canth., Carb-s., Carb-v., CARC., Chin., Clem., Cund., CON., *Crot-h.*, Elaps., Fuli., GRAPH., HYDR., Iod., Kali-ar., Kali-bi., KREOS., LACH, Lap-a., LYC., Mag-m., Merc., Merc-i-f., MURX., Nat-c., Nat-m., Nit-ac., PHOS., Phyt., Plat., *Rad-br.*, Rhus-t., *Sabin.*, Sang., *Scir.*, Sec., SEP., SIL., Staph., Sulph., Tarent., Thlas., THUJ., Visc., Zinc.
Cancer of Vagina	– Calc-ar., Graph., Hydr., KREOS., Nit-ac., Sep., Thuj.

OTHER TYPES

Encephaloma (Any Tumour of the Brain)	– Acet-ac., *Ars., Ars-i., Calc-c., Carb-ac., Carb-an.,* Caust., Kali-i., Kreos., Lach., Nit-ac., *Phos., Sil.,* Sulph., *Thuj.*
Epithelioma (Any Tumour– derived from epithelium)	*Arg-n., Ars.,* ARS-I., Bell., Bufo., *Clem.,* CON., *Cund.,* Hydr., Hydrc., Kali-s., Kreos., Lach., Lap-a., LYC., Merc-i-f., Phos., Phyt., Ran-b., Ran-s., *Sep.,* Sil., Thuj.
Lupus (Destructive type – of skin condition implying to local degeneration or slow Tubercular affection)	ARS., *Ars-i., Bar-c., Calc., Carb-ac., Carb-s., Carb-v., Cist.,* Graph., Hydr., Hydrc., Kali-bi., *Kali-chi., Kreos.,* LYC., Merc., Nat-m., Nit-ac., Phyt., *Psor.,* Rhus-t., Sep., *Sil., Thuj.,* Stap., Sulph.
Lupus., in rings	– *Sep.*
Melanoma	– *Arg-n.,* Card-m., *Lach.,* Ph-ac.
Open Cancers	– Apis, Carb-ac., Echi.
Sarcoma (A fleshy excrescence or Cancer of connective tissues)	– Ars., Bar-c. Carb-an., Lach., Lap-a.,Phos., Sil., Symph., *Thuj.*
Sarcoma - Lympho (i.e., Lymphoid tissue)	– Ars., Ars-i.
Sarcoma - Osteo	– Calc-f., Hecla., Symph.
Scirrhus (An indolent, hard Glandular Tumour often terminating in Cancer)	– *Alumn.,* Anac., Arg-m., Arn., Ars., Aster., Belli-p., Calc-s., CARB-AN., *Carb-s., Carb-v., Clem.,*

F-12

CON., *Graph., Hydr., Lap-al., Phos., Phyt.,* Sep., *Sil., Sulph.*

Cancer resulting from   –   Bell-p., Con.
contusion (Trauma)

In Cancer patients, to   –   Acon., Ph-ac., *Apis,* Anthraci.,
relieve pains   *Ars.,* Aster., Bry., *Calc-ac.,*
                               Calc-ar., Calc., Calc-ox.,
                               Card-m., *Carc., Ced.,* Cit-ac.,
                               Chol., Cinn., Clem., Cund.,
                               Con., Echi., Euphor., Graph.,
                               Hep., Hydrang., Hydr., Mag.-
                               p., Kali-p., Merc-i-f., Morph.,
                               Nit-ac., Op., Orni., Ova-t.,
                               Ox-ac., Phos-ac., Rad.,
                               Semp., Sil., Tarent-c.

In Cancerous conditions, – Ars., Ger., HOANG-NAN.
to stop bleeding, pain
and burning

CANCEROUS AFFECTIONS

Ulcer of Skin   –   *Ambraci., Anthr.,* ARS. Ars-i.,
                               ARS-S-F., *Aster.,* AUR-S.,
                               BUFO., Calc-s., Carb-ac.,
                               Carb-an., Carb-p., Carb-s.,
                               Con., Crot-c., *Ferr.,* Graph.,
                               HEP., Hipp., *Kali-i., Kreos.,*
                               Lach., LYC., *Lys., Merc.,* Mill.,
                               Nit-ac., *Petrol.,* Ph-ac., Phos.,
                               Phyt., Rhus-t., Sep., SIL.,
                               Spong., Staph., SULPH.,
                               Thuj.

ANTI-CANCEROUS REMEDIES

'A' Grade : Arg-n., Ars., Ars-i., *Asaf.,* Aur-m., Aur-m-n., Bism., Brom., Calc-ar., Carb-ac., Carb-an., Carc., Card-m. Carb-s., Carb-v., Chel., Chol., Cinn., Conch., Con., Echi., Hoang-n., Hydr., Iod., Iscador (Mistletos)., Kreos., Lach., Lap-a., Lyc., Mag-m., Medo., Merc-s., Nit-ac., Orni., Phos., Phyt., Rad-br., Scirr., Semp-v., *Sec.,* Sil., Stron-c., Syph., Tarent., Thuj., Thal., Visc-a., X-Ray.

'B' Grade : Acon-r., Alumn., Apis, Ambr., Anthraci., Ant-ar., Arg-m., Aster., Aur-ar., Aur-m., Bufo., Cadm., Calc-c., Calc-s., Chin., Cist., Clem., Crot-h., Fulig., Gal., Ger., Graph., Ham., Ign., Iris, Kali-c., Kali-ar., Kali-bi., Kali-i., Kali-chl., Kali-cy., Kali-p., Kali-s., Morph., Murx., Mur-ac., Mer-i-f., Nat-c., Nat-cac., Nat-m., Plb-i., Psor., Ran-b., Rob., Ruta, Scroph., Sep., Spong., Staph., Sulph., Zinc.[1]

Reference : Kent, Phatak and Boericke's Repertory, Barthel & Klunker's "Synthetic Repertory" including Clinical experience of Dr. A. H. Grimmer and the author.

---

1. Heartiest greetings to Dr. Nitratan Paul and Dr. ꜱatchidananda Choudhury for rendering hearty co-operation in writing this treatise.

9. AIDS

(Acquired Immuno-Deficiency Syndrome)
A NEW DISEASE OF THE CENTURY

INTRODUCTION

It is a disease of serious condition in which the body's immune system (its natural defence against infection and disease) is hampered. Such diseases are referred to as "opportunistic infections".

A few major "opportunistic" complications are :

(1) Bacterial : Mycobacterium avium – intracellular infections.

(2) Fungal : Candidiasis of mouth and oesophagus.

(3) Protozoal : Pneumocystis carinii – Toxoplasma gondii – diarrhoea due to Cryptosporidia species.

(4) Viral : Cytomegalovirus infections – Herpes simplex; localized Herpes zoster; Varicella zoster.

The sign and symptoms of opportunistic infection can be divided into :

(1) Central nervous system pattern.

(2) Gastro intestinal pattern.

(3) Pulmonary pattern.

(4) Fever of unknown etiology.

AETIOLOGY

AIDS is caused by a virus. It infects white cells in the blood. This virus is called human T - lymphotropic virus, type - III (HTLV - III); or AIDS related virus (ARV).

NATURE OF AIDS VIRUS

The virus launches a direct attack on helper T. cells (or T. Lymphocytes as they are also known), invading them in much the same way that the hepatitis virus homes on cells in the liver. Once encased in the T. cell, the AIDS virus prevents this vital cell from doing its job as that of the "initiator of cell immune system response." It turns the T. cell from being a lymphocyte on to being an AIDS-virus factory. The factory is extraordinarily efficient. The virus has a unique genetic component that allows it to reproduce itself a thousand times as fast as any other kind of virus. It explains why AIDS is such a devastating disease and why it can spread so fast. It is a peculiar feature of the disease that as it progresses, the helper T. cell disappear and so does the virus. By then, however, the patient is invariably beyond recovery.

WHERE WAS THE VIRUS DEVELOPED ?

The AIDS virus was developed in the laboratories of the PENTAGON in the year 1977. This is the conclusion of four scientists from different countries. They are Robert Stracher of U.S.A., Lilli Segal and Jacob Segal of France and Dr. John Seale of Britain.

DOES EVERYONE WITH THE VIRUS DEVELOPS AIDS ?

Not everyone with the virus develops AIDS or even falls sick. Most infected persons remains in good health.

Very few, only about 10% to 25% on the averages may develop illness varying in severity from mild to extremely serious.

INCUBATION PERIOD

The time between infection and the onset of symptoms seems to range from about 6 months to 5 years and possibly longer.

MODE OF TRANSMISSION

Although AIDS virus has been found in saliva and tears, no cases of transmission from exposure to these has been found. However, care should be taken when handling blood and tissue samples of patients at risk. Transmission requires intimate and not casual contact.

(1) Sexual contact.

(2) Sharing contaminated needles.

(3) Multiple transfusions of blood or blood products.

(4) Transmission from infected mother to child before, during or shortly after birth.

AIDS is transmitted through body fluids, i.e., blood, semen and not through casual normal social contact.

AIDS is not transmitted through sneezing or coughing.

AIDS is not transmitted through sitting near the AIDS patient.

It is not transmitted through kissing unless there is a cut or laceration on the lips, mouth or tongue.

AIDS is not contacted through shaking hands or secondhand garments.

Is blood donation dangerous ?

No. Blood collection centres use sterile equipment and disposable needles.

Does a condom offer any protection ?

As in the case of sexually transmissible diseases a condom may provide some protection against AIDS.

HIGH RISK GROUPS

1. Homosexual and bisexual men with multiple sexual partners.
2. Present or past drug abusers who use syringes for injecting drugs.
3. Persons with haemophilia or other coagulation disorders, i.e., people who receive transfusions of blood or blood products.
4. Babies born to mothers with AIDS.
5. Heterosexual contracts of someone with AIDS or at risk for AIDS.
6. Infants and children who have developed AIDS may have been exposed to HTLV III before or during birth or shortly thereafter.

AIDS primarily effects young adults It is not confined to homosexuals. It has the potential to affect a great many people.

If you are in a high risk group :

A. Have regular medical examination.
B. Avoid repeated exposure to sexually transmitted diseases.
C. Avoid sharing of needles to inject drugs.
D. Do not have more than one sexual partner.

E. Use condom.

F. Avoid oral and anal sex.

G. Don't share razors, tooth brushes, etc., which may be infected.

If you are seropositive – Always inform the health personnel whenever you need their help so that they can take appropriate precaution.

CLINICAL DIAGNOSIS

AIDS is difficult to diagnose. There is no single test for diagnosing AIDS. The presence of opportunistic diseases plus a positive test for antibodies to HTLV- III can be a positive diagnosis.

Presence of HTLV - III antibodies means that the person has been infected with the AIDS virus; it does not tell whether he is still infected.

ELISA (Enzyme Linked Immunosorbent Assay) Test indicates the presence of antibodies. More refined than ELISA (Which may send false alarms) is the Immuno-fluorescence Test, which identifies AIDS antibodies.

EARLY SIGNS AND SYMPTOMS

(1) Significant and unexplained weight loss.

(2) Swollen glands, usually in the neck, armpits or groin.

(3) Fever, night sweats and malaise.

(4) Persistent watery diarrhoea.

(5) Oral or/and oesophageal candidiasis.

(6) Tiredness/fatigue.

(7) Loss of appetite.

(8) Loss of memory.

Anyone with these symptoms which continue for more than two weeks should consult a physician.

Having any of these signs and symptoms does not necessarily confirm the diagnosis of AIDS. They may occur in other diseases as well.

PROGNOSIS

So far a full – blown case of AIDS has always proved fatal.

ASSOCIATED COMPLICATIONS

About 85% of the AIDS patients studied have had one or both of the two rare diseases.

1. Pneumocystis Carinii Pneumonia (PCP), a parasitic infection of the lungs.
2. Kaposi's Sarcoma (KS), a type of cancer. It occurs any where on the surface of the skin or in the mouth. There may also be Burkitts Tumour.

Other opportunistic infections include unusually *severe infections* with yeast, cytomegalovirus, herpesvirus, and parasites such as, *Toxoplasma* or *Cryptosporidia*. Milder infections with these organisms do not suggest immune deficiency.

AIDS RELATED COMPLEX

Most people develop a seemingly peaceful coexistence with the virus. They have symptoms or very minimal symptoms, but they have persistent infection and one probably persistently infectious to others. Another group suffers a mild version of immune – system depression, with symptoms that include malaise, weight loss, chills, fevers and swollen lymph nodes, persistent night sweats, diarrhoea. These syndrome, called AIDS – RELATED COMPLEX, or ARC (or Pre-AIDS), sometimes but not always develops into full-blown AIDS. Oral candidiasis or leukoplakic changes of tongue suggest overt AIDS in a year or so.

PREVENTION

Although research is under way, there is no vaccine for the prevention of AIDS till now. The following steps may be taken for its prevention :

(1) Do not have sexual contact with persons known or suspected of having AIDS.

(2) Homosexuals should be advised not to have different sexual partner.

(3) Do not have sex with multiple partners, or with persons who have had multiple partners.

(4) Checking up of all female and male prostitutes.

(5) If women are attacked with AIDS they should not carry children as there is sufficient evidence now to indicate that the infection is carried to foetus.

(6) Checking up of all haemophiliacs.

(7) Keeping check (by education/persuasion) on known drug dens having admixture of foreigners.

(8) Persons who are at high risk for having AIDS should not donate blood or semen.

(9) Do not abuse intravenous drugs; drug addicts must avoid sharing needles or syringes (boiling is no guarantee of sterility).

(10) Don't use inhalant nitrites (poppers).

(11) The high-risk group people must avoid

infections particularly those of sexually transmitted disease.

(12) Imported blood products should be certified as free from AIDS virus/antibody contamination.

(13) Surfaces which are contaminated with blood must be properly cleaned and decontaminated.

(14) All sorts of pseudo-cultural and denatural customs, habits and activists are the great hindrance for prevention and cure of any sickness.

HOMOEOPATHIC VIEW ON AIDS

As I mentioned earlier it is a *new venereal miasm,* two other venereal miasms, the syphilis and the sycosis are bacterial and new third, the AIDS is viral.

HOMOEOPATHIC TREATMENT

Though the miasm is new but its homoeopathic treatment is not new at all. As we do in all other diseases, acute or chronic, we are to record each and every case of AIDS patient according to the directives of the Organon and then we are to select medicine on the basis of totality of symptoms. Of course, all available medicines in our jurisdiction may not be sufficient for cure and prevention of patients infected with AIDS virus. Nosode of AIDS is absolutely necessary in these cases. Perhaps, that will be one of the very successful curative and preventive remedy against this dreadful disease. AIDS nosode will be a dependable weapon against AIDS as Syphilinum against syphilis, carcinocinum against cancer and Tuberculinum, Psorinum, Medorrhinum, etc., against tubercular, psoric and sycotic miasms. So, homoeopaths have nothing to be worried or bewildered with any so-called new disease. Rational and dialectical application of homoeopathic principles and doctrines, which are based on infallible laws of nature, on any disease state (acute or chronic, old or so-called new), if the same is curable must be cured with homoeopathic treatment.

Reference

1. Sputnik, March, 1987.
2. Paper, Published by US Department of Health and Human Services.
3. AIDS, General information, Indian Council of Medical Research, Ansari Nagar, New Delhi - 110029, April, 1986.
4. Ganasakti, 23.3.1987.
5. AIDS in INDIA, A Position Paper, Indian Council of Medical Research, New Delhi, August, 1986.

10. MIXED MIASMATIC STATES AND THEIR TREATMENT

We all know that there is no miasm-free man, or animal, or even plant in this universe. Not only that men are the victim of only one miasm, in most cases we find that several miasms are solely responsible for their diseases. Most of the complicated chronic 'diseases are the ultimate or end-product of mixed miasms. Generally we do not get the primary state of infection by different pathogens (microbs or miasms) at a time. What we usually get is the secondary or tertiary state where no pathogen is available in the laboratory test – excepting the pathogenic or toxic affect. Miasms are always separate, they cannot mix together. Only the miasmatic states may be intermingled. Hence, these states may be termed as *Mixed Miasmatic States.*

Now, what are the reasons that mankind have impregnated with so many pathogens at a time? Dr. Hahnemann states, "Psora is most ancient, most universal, most destructive and yet most misapprehended chronic miasmatic disease which for many thousands of years has disfigured and tortured mankind and which during the last centuries has become the mother of all the thousands of incredibly various (acute and) chronic (non-vernereal) diseases, by which the whole civilized human race on the inhabited globe is being more and more affected". This Psora or itch disease (i.e. disease due to pathogen or miasma of itch) had been forcibly suppressed for thousands of years before the discovery of homoeopathy within which it has seized the whole of mankind. So we get no man without *Psora.*

Similarly the miasm (or pathogen) of syphilis and gonorrhoea have infected all men and women involved in impure coition or conditions related with it for many thousand years. There was also no treatment for perfect cure of these venereal diseases except palliation or suppression before Dr. Hahnemann. Over and above, after the discovery of the vaccine against small pox Edward Jenner (1749-1843) in the eighteenth century, new drug – miasm, designated by Dr. Burnett as 'Vaccinosis', have been penetrated and afflicted human organisms which is most similar to sycotic miasm. Due to suppressive treatment by heroic medicines (like, sulpha drugs, chemotherapy, steroids and antibiotics, etc.) all the above miasmatic disease states have become more and more complicated day by day in one hand and more dangerous miasmatic diseases like Tuberculosis, cancer, AIDS etc. including unfavourable socio - economic - ecological conditions have plunged the mankind into the ocean of disaster on the other. So almost all men are basically affected with more than one pathogenic state nowadays. In this way we get the combined state of Psora and syphilis, or psora and sycosis, or psora and tuberculosis, or psora and cancer, or psora + syphilis + sycosis + tuberculosis + cancer. All the miasmatic states when combined present a picture which is too much complicated and very difficult to cure.

It would not be out of place to mention here that generally we get the following disease conditions when miasmatic states are combined :

Chronic ulceration, scrofulous conditions, hypertension and diabetes etc.	– due to psora - syphilis.
Asthma, warts, tumours, fleshy growths, rheumatism, rheumatic heart disease, etc.	– due to psora - sycosis.
Tubercular tendency	– due to psora - tuber-culosis.
Malignant tendency	– due to psora - cancer.
Psoriasis	– due to psora - syphilis - sycosis.
Cancerous diseases	– due to psora - syphilis - sycosis - tuberculosis - cancer.

In this connection it is to be noted that a patient may have two, three, four or five miasmatic states at a time. But one of thei 🤏 is very much active or dominant at one time. To start with the treatment we are to give more stress on that active, predominant state. Present conditions and totality of symptoms of the patient will dictate us to find out that predominant miasmatic state and to select medicine accordingly. Of course anti-mixed miasmatic medicine is to be selected in these cases.

From long-continued observation it will also be evident to all my follow brothers that as we hardly get any patient with single miasm or miasmatic state, we hardly get any medicine, especially the deep acting one, with single anti-miasmatic quality. Almost all deep acting remedies are anti-mixed miasmatic.

Now, as regards treatment, first of all we are to record the case in details, as we do in all other chronic

F-13

(or even acute) cases. From the history of the case we are to find out the peculiar, singular, uncommon and characteristic signs and symptoms on which we are to ascertain the totality of the symptoms. This will help us in identifying the miasmatic states and also what state is the predominant in the patient at the present phase. Suppose, amongst others 'Syphilitic state' is predominating. So, at the onset we are to select one 'A' grade anti-syphilitic medicine (say, Merc.) on the basis of the present totality of symptoms. This medicine is also anti-mixed miasmatic. This is to be continued as long as the patient continues all round improvement as per the tenets of the Organon sixth edition. After administering six courses of Merc. from LM/1 to LM/6 (or more or less than that) if it is observed that no further improvement follows, rather the patient is feeling indisposed otherwise, when we are to take the case afresh. After evolution of symptoms it is seen that the present totality of symptoms revealing the 'psoric state', i.e., dormant psora has come out after anti-syphilitic treatment. So the second prescription will be a 'A' grade anti-psoric medicine and it is also to be continued as before after which 'Sycotic State' may become in the forefront. Dormant or suppressed sycotic condition may be aroused after anti-psoric treatment. Hence, the 'third prescription will be a 'A' grade anti-sycotic medicine. In this way treatment and management of patients of mixed miasmatic states are to be followed. All 'A' grade anti-miasmatic medicines are also anti-mixed miasmatic ones as explained earlier.

The following mixed miasmatic disease conditions have been worked out by our honourable teachers, especially by Dr. P. Speight :

1. Bright's disease.

2. Chilblains.

3. Naevus or congenital markings of the skin

4. Elephantiasis.

5. Erysipelatous, carcinomatous conditions, epithelioma and lupus.

6. Psoriasis has been called the marriage of all the miasms, but its characteristic is predominantly psoric and sycotic.

7. Dropsy, anasarca, the formation of large tumours and various degenerative organic hypertrophies. They always have a tendency to expansion and in this way they deform nature's effort to ensure the continuation of life.

8. Ichthyosis, have the dryness of psora and squamae of syphilis and often moles and warty eruptions are present showing the sycotic element.

9. Hayfever which is one of the most troublesome condition we have as a base – the psoric, syphilitic and sycotic. The sycotic remains latent during the active period, but will come out later after proper treatment.

10. The fish scale eruption are also a combination of the three stigmata, with the dryness of the psora, the squamous character of the syphilis and the overgrowth of tissue or the thickened skin manifesta-tions of the sycosis.

11. Malignant cases have all the miasms present.

12. Degeneratives are sycotic or syphilitic or result from both (R).

13. When syphilis and sycosis are combined, these patients are sullen, smouldering, threatening to break out into dangerous manifestations (R).

14. Mental symptoms arising from moral insanity usually arise from a mixed miasm and sycosis combined with psora figures largely in the criminality of our country.

15. All toxic drugs become sooner or later prime distributor of psora or the chronic miasms in general but particularly psora.

16. Desires and aversions stand high in therapeutic as they are basic miasmatic symptoms next in importance to perverted mental phenomena in disease.

17. Cancerous affections, malignant growths and such diseases have as a rule all the miasms present, especially the sycotic and the tubercular combined. Psora can' never be left out of malignancies, no matter what other element may combine with it; it fathers them all.

We cannot expect any radical cure of complicated chronic diseases without anti-mixed miasmatic treatment. So this subject is of paramount importance in homoeopathy.

Homoeopathy can cure all curable states of ailments of human race with ease and economy and almost without side-effects especially with LM potencies. But it cannot cure the diseases which have reached their ultimates, where the vitality of the patient is irreparable. The ultimate and cancerous condition of the patients of mixed miasmatic states, especially in their ripe ages, where no real totality is available, are very hard to cure. So we should be conscious about our *limitations*.

ANTI-MIXED MIASMATIC REMEDIES

'A' Grade

Arg-met.	Med.	Phyt.	Thuj.
Aur.	Merc.	Psor.	Tub.
	Merc-i-f.		
Bac.	Merc-i-r.		
Calc-s.	Nit-ac.	Staph.	
Carc.		Sulph.	
		Syph.	
Lyc.			

Other Important Remedies

Aur-i.	Graph.	Lac-c.	Rad-br.
Aur-m.		Lach.	
Aur-s.	Hep.		Sars.
		Mang-ac.	Sep.
Benz-ac.	Iod.	Merc-c.	Sil.
		Mez.	Still.
Carb-v.	Kali-ar.		
Caust.	Kali-bi.	Nat-m.	Thyr.
Clem.	Kali-c.	Nat-s.	Tyl-i.
Con.	Kali-sal.		
	Kali-s.	Petr.	X-ray.
Ferr.		Phos.	
Fl-ac.		Ph-ac.	

11. IMPORTANCE OF 50 MILLESIMALS

The role of LM or 50 Millesimal scale of potency in homoeopathic treatment is also to be seriously considered.

Hahnemann had no other alternative but to revise his Organon, fifth Edition mainly for the following reasons :

1.   To hasten the process of cure. Gentle and rapid 'ideal of cure' is not possible by medicine of centesimal scale or it takes a long time in many cases.

2.   To avoid medicinal aggravation. The undesirable medicinal aggravation comes even after the well-selected medicine is applied especially in weak patients, regarding which Hahnemann stated, "...furious, even dangerous, violence."

3.   Even single dose of high potency continues to act for a long time.

4.   Repetition of doses is not possible even if there are remnant of symptoms of disease in consequence of which the patient suffers for a long time.

5.   The problems of application of doses and potencies still create chaos and confusion throughout the homoeopathic world.

6.   If the selection of medicine is wrong, then after application of high potency of centesimal scale the disease condition becomes more worse.

7. So, "the highest ideal of cure" according to aphorism 2 of the Organon could not be properly materialized with centesimal potency.

But all the above problems have almost been scientifically solved with LM potency of the Organon, sixth edition. Now, we can easily avail the following advantages of the 50 millesimal potency over the centesimal.

1. The latent and indwelling essence of medicinal substances develop to their fullest extent, so also the qualitative transformation in their higher form and in action these are more powerful. Hahnemann stated, "highest development of power and mildest action."

2. Medicine of this potency is milder in reaction. It can be safely applied even in the most deplorable case without fear of dangerous and violent medicinal aggravation.

3. It can be repeated if and when necessary. Even the medicines of long – continued action may be administered safely.

4. It cures both acute and chronic patients in surprisingly quickest possible time if applied by olfaction without any aggravation.

5. This potency renders full freedom to both physicians and patients from the tyranny of centesimal potency. If the selection is found to be wrong, new well-selected medicine may be administered without antidoting previous one.

6. Patients who have not been cured completely by the higher and highest degrees of centesimal scale recovers only by a few courses of medicine of this new scale.

7. By the medicines of this new scale rapid cure of all curable acute, severe and chronic cases are possible which is the greatest reward to the homoeopathic profession.

8. (a) Only with these medicine, period of treatment can be diminished to one-half, one-quarter or even still mitigated.

(b) Only medicines of this new system can face boldly any challenge with the so-called modern medicines in regard to quickest recovery.

For the circumstances as stated above great Hahnemann had to discard Organon, fifth edition with its centesimal scale of potencies and developed it to the LM potencies in sixth edition. What Hahnemann stated regarding the rejection of the Organon, fifth edition is of paramount importance :

"What I said in the Fifth edition of the Organon, in a long note this paragraph in order to prevent these undesirable reactions of the vital energy, was all that the experience I then had justified. But during the last four or five years, however, all these difficulties are wholly solved by my new, altered but perfected method."

(Foot-note to Aph.246.
Organon, Sixth Edition.)

It is expected that all rational and dynamic physicians will endeavour heartily to put LMs into their practice for the sake of rapid and gentle recovery of their patients. It is the latest and most mature scientific contribution of our great teacher Dr. S. Hahnemann on the basis of his life-long research and experimentation.'

For detailed *information* as regards preparation and application of LM potencies learned readers may kindly take trouble to consult the "Organon, Sixth Edition "by Dr. Hahnemann and "50 Millesimal Potency in Theory and Practice" by the author.

CONCLUSION

All the enormous advancement in the field of bio-chemistry, genetic science and engineering, cellular and molecular pathology assists us in easy recognition of all the series of symptoms and their qualitative degree of each miasm. Now we can more surely and unmistakably identify and correct the psoric deficiency, syphilitic dysfunction, sycotic hypertrophy, tubercular destruction and cancerous degeneration in all the given and collected symptoms of our patients.

I earnestly hope that the indications compiled and written in this book will facilitate and simplify the classification of all the symptoms for each of the Hahnemannian doctrine of miasms including new ones.

We all are well aware of the fact that susceptibility or the inner contradictions are primary causes of all diseases. These pathogens (micro-organisms and viruses) or miasms are the source of primary or fundamental causes of diseases. On the other hand, it is also a fact that without favourable condition, e.g., exciting and maintaining causes, which may be considered as the secondary contradictions, only fundamental causes cannot produce diseases unconditionally. So, we are to evaluate both the primary and secondary causes, e.g., inner and outer contradictions of diseases accurately to restore the sick to health, the ONLY CALLING OF ALL PHYSICIANS. These indications may be useful to my brothers in the profession to ascertain and identify the primary causes including necessary hints for their suitable treatment. And our proper consciousness about the tyranny of the class society will inspire us to be a staunch fighter against secondary causes (e.g., unfavourable and detrimental socio-economic and ecological hazards). For a healthy, happy and prosperous human society we are greatly in need of a world free from diseases (as far as practicable), wars, weapons and exploitations. For this reason great Hahnemann invites us not only to become rational physician but also to be preserver of health. I want to conclude with his invaluable saying :

"He is likewise a preserver of health if he knows the things that derange health and cause disease, and how to remove them from persons in health."

REFERENCES

1. Hahnemann, S.   :   The Chronic Diseases, Their Nature and Their Homoeopathic Cure.

2. Hahnemann, S.   :   The Organon of Medicine, Sixth Edition.

3. Hahnemann, S.   :   Lesser Writings.

4. Close, Stuart   :   The Genius of Homoeopathy.

5. Speight, Phyllis   :   A Comparison of the Chronic Miasms.

6. Roberts, H.A.   :   The Principles and Arts of Cure by Homoeopathy.

7. Ortega, P.S.   :   Notes on Miasms.

8. Kent, J.T.   :   Lectures on Homoeopathic Philosophy.

9. Allen, J.H.   :   The Chronic Miasms.

10. A Team of Experienced Teachers   :   Short Notes on Chronic Diseases and Theory of Miasms.

11. Fortier-Bernoville   :   Syphilis and Sycosis.

12. Boenninghausen, C.M.F.   :   The Lesser Writings.

13. Hughes, Richard   :   The Principles and Practice of Homoeopathy, P-I + P-Il.

14. Sarkar, B.K.   :   Introduction and Commentary

on the Organon.

15. Kanjilal, J.N. : Writings on Homoeopathy.

16. Choudhury, H.M. : Miasm and Bacteriology "Homoeo - Samiksha", 3rd Year, 4th Issue.

17. Clark, J.H. : Constitutional Medicine.

18. Banerjee, D.N. : Text Book of Pathology.

19. Vinogradov, A.V. : Differential Diagnosis of Internal Diseases.

20. Vithoulkas, George: The Science of Homoeopathy.

21. Agrawal, Y.R. : A Comparative Study of Chronic Miasm.

22. Tyler, M.L. : Hahnemann's Conception of Chronic Disease, as by Parasitic Micro-Organisms.

AUTHOR

DR. HARIMOHON CHOUDHURY

SHORT BIO-DATA

EXPERIMENTER, EXPOUNDER & PIONEER	: 50 Millesimal Scale of Potency.
PROFOUNDER	: Dialectical Materialistic Interpretation of Homoeopathy
TRANSLATOR	: Organon Sixth Edition in Bengali.
AUTHOR	: 1. 50 Millesimal Potency in Theory and Practice.
	2. Indications of Miasm.
	3. Ignatia (Bengali)
	4. Medorrhinum (Bengali)
	5. Homoeopathy in the light of Dialectic Materialism (Bengali)
	6. Tuberculinum (Bengali)
	7. Case Record Book (Bengali & English).
CHIEF ADVISOR	: Homoeo - Samiksha.
ADVISOR	: Hahnemann Ke Raste.
FOUNDER MEMBER	: P.H.C. SAMITY.
MEMBER EDITORIAL BOARD	: Bijnanmanas

PROFESSOR	:	Organon of Medicine, Bengal Allen Medical Institute, International Training Division, Calcutta.
	:	Organon of Medicine, C. H. M. College.
CHIEF EDITOR	:	"Samabidhan" and "Ajker Homoeo Pragati."
FOUNDER G. SECRETARY	:	B. Homoeopathic Parisad.